# Praise for In

"This series provides a practical and foc
today." – John V. Biernacki, Partner, Joi

*Inside the Minds* draws from the collective experience of the best professionals. The books are informative from an academic, and, more importantly, practical perspective. I highly recommend them." – Keith M. Aurzada, Partner, Bryan Cave LLP

"Aspatore's *Inside the Minds* series provides practical, cutting edge advice from those with insight into the real world challenges that confront businesses in the global economy." – Michael Bednarek, Partner, Shearman & Sterling LLP

"What to read when you want to be in the know—topical, current, practical, and useful information on areas of the law that everyone is talking about." – Erika L. Morabito, Partner, Patton Boggs LLP

"Some of the best insight around from sources in the know" – Donald R. Kirk, Shareholder, Fowler White Boggs PA

"The *Inside the Minds* series provides a unique window into the strategic thinking of key players in business and law." – John M. Sylvester, Partner, K&L Gates LLP

"Comprehensive analysis and strategies you won't find anywhere else." – Stephen C. Stapleton, Of Counsel, Dykema Gossett PLLC

"The *Inside the Minds* series is a real hands-on, practical resource for cutting edge issues." – Trey Monsour, Partner, Haynes and Boone LLP

"A tremendous resource, amalgamating commentary from leading professionals that is presented in a concise, easy to read format." – Alan H. Aronson, Shareholder, Akerman Senterfitt

"Unique and invaluable opportunity to gain insight into the minds of experienced professionals." – Jura C. Zibas, Partner, Lewis Brisbois Bisgaard & Smith LLP

"A refreshing collection of strategic insights, not dreary commonplaces, from some of the best of the profession." – Roger J. Magnuson, Partner, Dorsey & Whitney LLP

"Provides valuable insights by experienced practitioners into practical and theoretical developments in today's ever-changing legal world." – Elizabeth Gray, Partner, Willkie, Farr & Gallagher LLP

"This series provides invaluable insight into the practical experiences of lawyers in the trenches." – Thomas H. Christopher, Partner, Kilpatrick Stockton LLP

# ASPATORE

Aspatore Books, a Thomson Reuters business, exclusively publishes C-Level executives and partners from the world's most respected companies and law firms. Each publication provides professionals of all levels with proven business and legal intelligence from industry insiders—direct and unfiltered insight from those who know it best. Aspatore Books is committed to publishing an innovative line of business and legal titles that lay forth principles and offer insights that can have a direct financial impact on the reader's business objectives.

Each chapter in the *Inside the Minds* series offers thought leadership and expert analysis on an industry, profession, or topic, providing a future-oriented perspective and proven strategies for success. Each author has been selected based on their experience and C-Level standing within the business and legal communities. *Inside the Minds* was conceived to give a first-hand look into the leading minds of top business executives and lawyers worldwide, presenting an unprecedented collection of views on various industries and professions.

INSIDE THE MINDS

# Business Due Diligence Strategies

*Leading Lawyers on Conducting*
*Due Diligence in Today's M&A Deals*

## 2014 EDITION

ASPATORE

# CONTENTS

Chelsea A. Grayson                                    7
*Partner,* Loeb & Loeb LLP
*THE IMPACT OF, AND CERTAIN TRENDS
IN, MODERN DUE DILIGENCE REVIEWS*


Jennifer L. Vergilii and Neil J. Whitford          17
*Partners,* Calfee Halter & Griswold LLP
*KEEPING UP WITH THE TIMES: RECENT
DEVELOPMENTS IN DUE DILIGENCE*


Gerard O'Connor                                     31
*Partner,* Saul Ewing LLP
*EVOLVING IP AND INTERNATIONAL
CONCERNS CONTINUALLY ADD NEW
CHALLENGES FOR M&A ATTORNEYS*


James A. Butz                                       49
*Member,* Frost Brown Todd LLC
*WE DISCLOSED WHAT? SELLER STRATEGIES
TO MITIGATE RISKS ASSOCIATED WITH EVOLVING
INFORMATION EVALUATION TECHNIQUES*


Michael G. Platner and Solomon B. Zoberman         57
*Partners,* Lewis Brisbois Bisgaard & Smith LLP
*TEN IMPEDIMENTS TO A SUCCESSFUL DUE
DILIGENCE PROCESS AND KEY TRENDS
IMPACTING TODAY'S M&A DEALS*


Appendices                                          79

# The Impact of, and Certain Trends in, Modern Due Diligence Reviews

Chelsea A. Grayson

*Partner*

Loeb & Loeb LLP

ASPATORE

## Introduction

This chapter will provide insight and guidance as to certain key issues and considerations that can arise in a modern due diligence review, as those issues and considerations impact or inform upon mergers & acquisitions involving a private target. Practitioners will find this discussion most relevant in the context of middle market, domestic or cross-border mergers & acquisitions.

### Impact of Modern Diligence Reviews on Transaction Process and Pace

When it comes to the impact a modern due diligence review has on transaction process and pace, the stakes have never been higher for sellers. Traditionally, buyers have run their diligence reviews on a parallel track with the drafting and negotiation of the definitive documentation. So, at middling or even later points along the deal timeline, buyers use flaws that they discover to ratchet down the purchase price or to negotiate specific protective indemnity obligations.

Buyers today break from that tradition when they can, in an effort to aggressively reduce deal process-related expenses. A growing trend among buyers is to delay the drafting and negotiating of definitive documentation while they engage in a robust diligence review. When they reach a point in the diligence review where they are more confident that they have an attractive, viable deal and certainty to close, only then will they turn to documents. Alternatively, if buyers have less money, time, and effort invested in a transaction because they have focused only on diligence, then once they have flushed out issues in performing a robust diligence review, they have more flexibility to walk away from a deal.

Traditionally, buyers rarely terminated a deal when they discovered issues, because of the general belief that most flaws can be effectively addressed by employing any number of protective provisions (a position buttressed by difficulty in justifying a termination in light of the money, time, and effort already invested in negotiating the transaction). Buyers today are becoming increasingly less cavalier about consummating a transaction involving a troubled target.

For sellers involved in deals where buyers refuse to turn to documentation until substantial diligence has progressed, the good news is that they are less likely to be approached with eleventh hour proposals regarding specific indemnity obligations or a purchase price reduction. The bad news is that sellers will potentially spend a significant amount of money, time, and effort in responding to a fulsome diligence review that does not ultimately yield a closed transaction.

So, it is imperative that sellers perform internal diligence and put their house in order as much as possible prior to going to market. This can reduce the time it will take to get through a diligence process but will also reduce the risk that a buyer will find a reason to back out, or propose onerous indemnity obligations or a reduced purchase price.

But sellers should not stop at doing what they can to beautify the target for the market. Sellers should also be prepared to offer comprehensive disclosures and explanations for problems that they have not been able to fix (or that they have chosen not to fix). In fact, best practices dictate that sellers exercise a preemptive strike and post these explanatory points in the data room at the outset of the process, so that a buyer does not need to discover the issue on its own. In this way, the sellers look knowledgeable, organized, and proactive, which inspires confidence by the buyer in the sell-side team and the target.

### Effects of the Foreign Corrupt Practices Act

On the buy side of acquisitions, modern diligence has been most significantly impacted by the increased enforcement activity under the Foreign Corrupt Practices Act, and by the repeated admonitions of the Department of Justice (DOJ) and the Securities & Exchange Commission (SEC) to conduct aggressive FCPA due diligence prior to mergers and acquisitions.[1]

---

[1] 15 U.S.C. §§ 78dd-1 *et seq.* (West).

By way of brief refresher, the FCPA prohibits a US company from bribing a foreign official to induce the foreign official to assist in obtaining or retaining work for the US company. There are stiff civil monetary penalties for violations, and individuals associated with an offending entity can face criminal charges, which can lead to imprisonment and additional fines.

Entities looking to acquire US businesses with even minimal operations abroad, or US entities looking to acquire foreign targets (among other sorts of buyers), should be on heightened alert and should carefully scrutinize the target's operations and accounting practices for violations.

Luckily, the SEC and DOJ have provided some guidance for acquisitive companies looking to stay in line with the FCPA as they go through their diligence reviews. In November 2012, the SEC and DOJ published their resource guide to the US Foreign Corrupt Practices Act 29. While it does not purport to be a comprehensive, step-by-step instruction manual, it does give a good illustration of best practices and is certainly the best starting point for those unfamiliar with the process of diligence in this area.

A thorough risk-based FCPA and anti-corruption diligence review on targets will include the following sorts of investigations and inquiries:

1. Does the target maintain a code of conduct and have FCPA compliance policies or procedures in place, including internal accounting controls? Are these controls state-of-the-art or do they need polishing? Are they functioning effectively or should they be further tailored to fit the specific business (and risks) at issue? The 2012 guide goes into further detail as to what makes for a modern and effective compliance policy, for those readers who want to take a closer look.

2. Do the policies mentioned in number 1, above, require the target to diligence parties with whom it contracts, such as consultants, sales representatives, distributors, commission agents, and parties with whom the target has a joint venture in place?

3. Do the target's employees actually comply with the policies mentioned in number 1? One way to figure this out is to do on-

the-ground interviews with management, employees, and even some or all of these third parties. Include in this process, interviews with key personnel, such as the general counsel or other in-house legal counsel, and management who have leadership roles in the sales and the internal audit departments.

4. Does the target conduct random audits of its contractual relationships (and involved third parties) to flush out corruption-related issues?

5. What is the target's customer base? Is it largely foreign state-owned or state-controlled entities? Or are the target's contracts or business generally subject to government approval or regulation?

6. Thoroughly review the target's financial and sales data for evidence of bribes that might have been mischaracterized. Can you spot extraordinary or high commission payments or consulting fees? Has the target made unusual travel or entertainment expenditures? Are there unexplained petty cash withdrawals? Check for write-offs, rebates, and discounts as well.

7. Have foreign governmental authorities conducted (or are they currently conducting) audits or investigations on or including the target related to bribery or corruption?

By far, the biggest impact the FCPA has had on modern diligence is that it has extended the diligence period past the closing and has incorporated a continuing diligence review throughout the post-closing integration process. This can include, among other things, conducting FCPA audits immediately after the closing. This obviously increases the legal spend involved in a transaction, so buyers should factor in that additional expense when projecting deal budgets.

Significantly, the more robust the diligence and integration process, the less likely an acquirer will take on successor liability, even if the illegal activity continues after the deal has consummated (assuming the acquirer was not aware of and did not condone the continuing activity, and assuming the buyer promptly discloses to the government any violations and potential violations). In light of how severe the penalties can be for a violation, and in light of the additional scrutiny the government is placing on this area now, this area of diligence has taken on a much higher priority than ever before (in applicable circumstances).

**Social Media Review as Part of the Diligence Process**

Modern buyers must include a review of a target's social media presence and policies in the diligence process. A buyer can learn a lot from social media about the target's reputation and goodwill, its customers, public relations and customer satisfaction, marketing practices, and its general business activities.

A buyer should get a clear and comprehensive understanding about how the target uses social media. At a basic level, a diligence request list in this area would ask for the target's social media policy (including an explanation of the target's monitoring and enforcement policies and practices, particularly in respect of third-party postings), a list of all social media sites the target has used or currently uses, the username and password information in respect to each such platform, and a list of all people and entities that have access to the target's social media accounts. The buyer should also confirm that the target has effective and current releases in place in respect to all content and images or videos posted on social media platforms, or elsewhere on its behalf. Finally, the buyer should speak with the target's social media officer to fill in the gaps and provide a fleshed-out understanding of the role of social media for the target's business and operations, and what glitches there have been and typically exist in this context.

A bit of sleuthing is necessary here as well. The buyer should try to discern (in a manner consistent with privacy laws) how the target's employees use social media on their own time in ways that impact the target. A buyer can learn a lot about the target's culture and internal synergies (both of which can impact company performance) from what its employees say about it online.

**Privacy Concerns; Hindrance to Diligence Process**

Buyers must be aware of data privacy laws that apply to the various individuals they are attempting to diligence. Diligence reviews that focus on individuals arise in many contexts. An FCPA diligence will necessarily involve a diligence review of the parties the target has contractual or business relationships with, as discussed earlier. A buyer might want to do background checks on the key personnel or shareholders of the target. A buyer will want to understand the customer or client base of the target. A buyer might want to understand overarching statistics and information about a health care target's patients.

Fundamentally, privacy laws are concerned with targets disclosing personal or identifying information about their employees, customers, clients, or, as applicable, patients. This ranges from obvious pieces of information, such as addresses and social security numbers, to health-related information and specific pension-related information. Basically, privacy laws target information that a third party could reverse engineer and identify the individual being diligenced.

Lawyers need to manage their buy-side clients' expectations in the diligence process, to the extent that privacy laws are a factor. Buyers might only be able to obtain redacted versions of lists of employees, job titles, and compensation information or redacted versions of patient or client lists. Redacted documentation helps the sellers retain the anonymity of the information being provided, so that the data cannot be traced back to specific individuals. Generally, however, buyers will still be able to glean useful data from these redacted documents.

Aside from determining what actual data a buyer can obtain when privacy laws are implicated, the first question is: What procedure do the applicable data privacy laws require to obtain that information? Generally, these legal schemes require that the individual who is the subject of the diligence review be notified (and in some cases, the individual must provide consent before the investigation can proceed). This obligation can fall on the buyer, even if the information is coming directly from the target (because the buyer is the party doing the investigating). The notice obligation can be quite onerous in terms of the sort of information that must be disclosed to the recipient— particularly if the parties are sensitive about keeping the existence of the deal and its terms confidential (which is usually the case). For example, the notice might need to explain why the individual is being diligenced, the identity of the buyer, whether third parties will see the diligence results and whether the individual has a right to review and potentially correct the information discovered.

Buyers should also carefully review the target's privacy compliance program to determine whether it is missing vital or legally required provisions, whether it is not quite state-of-the-art or whether the target's employees adhere to the program. Along these lines, buyers should inquire as to what sort of data the target generally collects in the ordinary course of its business, what the target's direct marketing policies and practices are, and what data security breach incidents have occurred and how have they been handled, among other things.

**Conclusion**

Both sellers and buyers must be on heightened alert when addressing modern due diligence reviews. Modern due diligence impacts deal process and pace in ways that break from tradition. Best practices dictate that sellers begin to prepare for the diligence review before the target is introduced to the market, both by resolving issues and by getting their arms around flaws that cannot be fixed. Buyers should be prepared to invest money, time, and effort on a fulsome FCAP-related diligence—one that can continue in the post-closing transition period. Buyers should also include in their diligence request checklists a set of inquiries related to social media. Finally, buyers should understand that sellers might be required to submit responses to diligence inquiries that are redacted or modified in some way, to account for privacy concerns and to comply with related laws; buyers should be flexible and try to glean what useful information they can, while understanding that some information might not be accessible until after the closing.

**Key Takeaways**

- Because a current trend is for buyers to hold off on drafting and negotiating definitive deal documentation until they have substantially completed their diligence review, sellers should invest time, money, and effort on internal diligence prior to going to market.
- Entities looking to acquire US businesses with even minimal operations abroad, or US entities looking to acquire foreign targets (among other sorts of buyers), should be on heightened alert and should carefully scrutinize the target's operations and accounting

practices for violations to avoid enforcement actions under the Foreign Corrupt Practices Act.

• Buyers should add social media-related inquiries and investigations to their list of important areas to diligence.

• Buyers should be aware that privacy concerns might cause a hindrance in the sorts of information accessible to buyers in pre closing diligence reviews.

*Chelsea A. Grayson is a partner in the Corporate Practice Group at Loeb & Loeb LLP in Los Angeles. She focuses primarily on mergers and acquisitions, corporate governance and counseling, joint ventures and strategic alliances. She has experience in a broad array of industries, including new media, infrastructure/engineering and construction, building products, technology, manufacturing, aerospace and defense, mining and drilling, alternative energy, health care, retail, sports, music, and entertainment. Prior to joining Loeb & Loeb, Ms. Grayson was a partner in the Mergers and Acquisitions Practice Group at Jones Day in Los Angeles.*

*Ms. Grayson recently was a recipient of the 40 Under 40 Recognition Award from the* M&A Advisor *and was also named one of "L.A.'s Top 40 Dealmakers" in the* Los Angeles Business Journal's *"Who's Who in L.A. Law." She is also listed in* The Legal 500 US In M&A: Middle Market. *Ms. Grayson has published articles in* The Deal Magazine and Healthcare Review. *Ms. Grayson is a faculty member for CLE provider Lawline, and frequently lectures on M&A or participates on M&A panels (most recently for Lincoln International, Martindale-Hubbell, and Strafford Publications).*

# Keeping Up with the Times: Recent Developments in Due Diligence

Jennifer L. Vergilii and Neil J. Whitford

*Partners*

Calfee Halter & Griswold LLP

ASPATORE

## Introduction

"Due diligence" refers to the process of investigating the business, legal, and financial health of an entity so that a buyer, lender or other investor can make an informed investment decision with regard to a business relationship. Information obtained through due diligence is used to assess the possible risks and rewards of a transaction, and often is relied on during the negotiation of the economic and other terms of a deal. This chapter focuses on due diligence conducted in connection with the purchase of a business.

Buyers use information obtained during the due diligence process to negotiate the specific terms of the purchase agreement. For example, a prospective buyer of a business may require the seller to correct an environmental, tax or other legal compliance issue prior to the closing, or the buyer may demand full protection/indemnification (without any time or monetary limits) with respect to that issue. A thorough due diligence investigation is vital to reconciling the proposed purchase price with the value of the business being purchased. Due diligence also helps to identify the impediments to, and the hidden costs of, a proposed transaction.

A purchase agreement generally will include a wide range of representations and warranties regarding the target business. Often, a seller will conduct its own due diligence with regard to the business being sold to gather the necessary information to make appropriate disclosures to the buyer in the purchase agreement. Those disclosures typically are contained in "disclosure schedules" to the purchase agreement. Disclosures often represent exceptions to the general statements being made in the representations and warranties. For example, a purchase agreement may include a representation by the seller that, except as set forth in the disclosure schedules, the target is not subject to any pending or threatened lawsuits or other claims—with any such claims being summarized in the disclosure schedules. The prospective buyer will use the seller's disclosure schedules to verify the accuracy and completeness of the seller's representations and warranties against the buyer's own diligence findings. A buyer should not, however, rely on the information in the disclosure schedules as a substitute for its own diligence investigation, but rather should use that information as a method to confirm its due diligence findings.

Most due diligence reviews begin with the development of a due diligence checklist. That checklist includes a list and description of the information and documents the buyer and its advisers (including legal counsel) want to review. The buyer, with input from its attorneys and other representatives, should tailor the checklist to suit the transaction at hand. That tailoring may involve specific references to key elements of the target's business. Depending on the type of business conducted by the target, additional diligence may be warranted in certain areas. For example, if the target is a manufacturer, there may be product liability concerns; where chemicals are used in a manufacturing process, environmental compliance may be of particular concern; and if the target engages in operations in multiple jurisdictions, additional tax-related diligence may be appropriate.

Due diligence is a highly interdisciplinary process involving many areas of specialization. Although a transactional lawyer typically quarterbacks the legal due diligence review, a thorough review requires input from other lawyers and advisors with different expertise, including advisors with knowledge about financial, tax, accounting, environmental, real estate, employee benefits, and intellectual property matters. Because the due diligence process is so interdisciplinary, teamwork and effective organization are critical.

**Social Media and Due Diligence**

Long gone are the days when a buyer would rely solely on information provided by the seller to conduct its due diligence review. Buyers are now much more proactive in conducting their due diligence. For example, lawyers and other due diligence advisors are becoming savvier about social media, which is an increasingly important tool in today's M&A due diligence process. Just as "data rooms" housing due diligence documents have evolved from dedicated office spaces to virtual databases, today, with the click of a button, the Internet can be searched to reveal significant information about a target and its key executives. Internet research also can provide a potential buyer with insight into how customers, suppliers, and competitors perceive a target. Whether such Internet information is fact or fiction, real or perceived, the challenge is weeding through the information to obtain an accurate picture of the target.

Fasken Martineau's 2013 Social Media M&A Survey[1] indicated that 48 percent of primarily US-based M&A executives used social media to research companies involved in transactions. Interestingly, that Fasken report was conducted prior to an April 2013 report[2] from the US Securities and Exchange Commission that provided guidance for communicating material, non-public information by means of social media platforms. In that report, the SEC approved the use of social media outlets, such as Twitter, to announce key information, provided investors are first informed of what social media sites would be used. That report quelled concerns that the use of such outlets for disclosure might violate Regulation Fair Disclosure (Reg FD),[3] a rule that requires companies to disclose material information publicly. One can only presume that the guidance provided in the 2013 SEC report will accelerate the trend of companies using social media as a disclosure outlet.

Publicly traded companies need to be aware of other laws that may be implicated by the use of social media sites. For example, providing information about a potential M&A transaction via a social media outlet may be deemed a "solicitation" of proxies that would be subject to Rule 14-a-12 of the Securities and Exchange Act.[4] Likewise, Rule 165 of the Securities Act of 1933[5] could be implicated if a company uses a social media site to communicate information related to a business combination. Given the widespread use of social media sites,

---

[1] Fasken Marineau, *2013 Social Media M&A Survey*, (May 29, 2013), http://www.fasken.com/files/upload/Fasken-Martineau-2013-Mergers-and-Acquisitions-Social-Media-Survey.pdf.
[2] Report of Investigation Pursuant to Section 21(a) of the Securities Exchange Act of 1934: Netflix, Inc. and Reed Hastings, Release No. 69279.
[3] 17 C.F.R. § 243.100 *et seq.*
[4] 17 C.F.R. § 243.14a-12.
[5] 17 C.F.R. § 230.165.

both at work and privately by employees, public companies should educate their employees about relevant federal securities laws to avoid unintended violations.

Understanding the social media presence, policies, and enforcement of a target company is becoming an increasingly important goal of due diligence. You should be wary of using a "form" due diligence checklist that has not been updated to keep up with the increasing use of social media. For example, a comprehensive due diligence checklist should request a list of the social media outlets used by the target, the user names and passwords for such accounts, a list of which employees have access to and use such accounts, and an explanation of the company's use of such social media outlets. Obtaining an understanding of the breadth and depth of social media use by a target company will help the buyer to integrate the target into its social media marketing and disclosure policies after the closing.

A due diligence checklist also should request all policies of the target related to its employees' use of social media—after all, use of social media by employees, whether for personal or business use, may be a reflection on the target company. For example, are there restrictions on what an employee can post on his or her personal Facebook page? Also, does the company actively enforce its social media policies and, if so, what are the ramifications of noncompliance?

Some of the most common issues faced by companies due to the rise of social media include the dissemination of confidential information of the employer, disparaging comments about the employer or colleagues, and inappropriate photos, behavior or comments that negatively reflect on the user's employer. Understanding a target's risk profile, as it relates to social media usage by its employees, will help the buyer assess the overall value of the transaction.

The inclusion of social media as part of a due diligence review, and the use of social media to disclose actual and potential transactions, are on the rise. Further changes in technology and the law no doubt will impact future practices in this area.

## Use of Insurance in M&A Transactions

Since the collapse of the financial markets in 2008, the gap has widened between what buyers want to pay and what sellers are willing to accept as a purchase price. That valuation disconnect, coupled with buyers' increased reliance on due diligence and general reluctance to assume unknown liabilities, sometimes makes it difficult to close a transaction. M&A insurance products can be used as a tool to bridge the gap on those valuation and risk allocation issues. Insurance for M&A transactions can take many forms. The most common types of transactional insurance products are (i) representation and warranty insurance, which provides coverage for losses associated with a breach of a representation or warranty in the purchase agreement; (ii) tax liability insurance, which provides coverage for unpaid taxes and penalties; (iii) legal contingency insurance, which covers successor liability exposure; and (iv) environmental liability insurance, which provides remediation coverage for preexisting conditions (whether known or unknown) and third party liability.

In the past, buyers often were reluctant to rely on M&A insurance products, in part due to uncertainty as to whether any related claims would be covered/honored by the insurance carriers. But in today's sellers' market, transactional insurance risk products are becoming more commonly accepted—especially in middle market transactions. The "sweet spot" for M&A insurance seems to be transactions with a purchase price between $15 million and $1.5 billion.[6]

When a buyer and seller agree to the terms of an M&A transaction, those terms typically include indemnification by the seller in the event of a breach of any of its representations or warranties. In some transactions, the buyer requires that the seller escrow a portion of the purchase price to cover such indemnity claims. Representation and warranty insurance can be very attractive to sellers because it can protect them from post-closing indemnification liabilities. Such insurance also can be an effective tool for prospective buyers in an auction setting, by allowing them to offer lower seller indemnification

---

[6] Dave Lindorff, *Minimizing M&A Risks*, TREASURY & RISK MAGAZINE (Nov. 4, 2012).

exposure and thereby making their bids more attractive. Premiums for these insurance products vary, depending on the type of coverage, cap on coverage, deductible, risks associated with the target business, and other factors. However, a premium in the range of 2 to 4 percent of the coverage amount, with a deductible of 1 to 3 percent of transaction value, is not uncommon.[7]

By way of example, one of the authors of this chapter recently had success in assisting a client, the seller of a company with a messy environmental history, in obtaining coverage in connection with a $25 million divestiture. By the time the insurance carrier was approached, several buyers had already walked away from the transaction due to environmental concerns. Phase I and phase II environmental studies conducted during the due diligence process did not alleviate environmental concerns—instead, they opened up a Pandora's box of additional issues. The insurance carrier was able to issue a $10 million pollution policy that covered both the seller and the buyer for a ten-year term at a premium of approximately $220,000. The seller paid for the insurance and was able to divest the business, knowing that it would retain the purchase price received, rather than using those funds to cover potential environmental claims by the buyer after the closing. Likewise, the buyer took comfort in the knowledge that it was not walking into an unfunded contingent liability. There is no doubt that environmental insurance was the M&A tool that got this transaction over the finish line.

## Increased Focus on Certain Due Diligence Areas

*Intellectual Property*

Leaders of companies often cite intellectual property (IP) as a key driver of their future growth. For many target companies, IP is one of their most valuable assets. If anything, the importance of IP to companies is likely to increase in the coming years.[8] Given this environment, it is not at all surprising that a major focus of current due diligence investigations is the IP of the target business. At a

---

[7] *Id.*

[8] 2011 and 2012 World Intellectual Property Reports (World Intellectual Property Organization).

minimum, an IP due diligence review should cover all of the target company's registered IP (i.e., patents, trademarks, trade names, and copyrights) and pending applications, trade secrets, know-how, and licenses and other IP-related agreements.

Depending on the importance of IP to the buyer, the scope of the IP review may be quite broad, potentially including a non-infringement analysis of the target's main product lines, a validity analysis of the target's key patents, and/or a competitive landscape patent review. As to trade secrets, there is a perception in some quarters that trade secrets have become even more valuable following the passage of the Leahy-Smith America Invents Act.[9] However, care must be taken to ensure that the due diligence process does not inadvertently undermine the protected status of any confidential information as a trade secret.

*Foreign Corrupt Practices Act*

The level of enforcement of the Foreign Corrupt Practices Act of 1977[10] (FCPA) has varied over the years since its enactment, depending on the enforcement priorities of different presidential administrations. Over the past few years, however, it has been vigorously enforced. One of the key provisions of the FCPA is a prohibition on the offer or payment of a bribe to a non-US government official to obtain a contract or gain some other business advantage. Penalties can range from civil penalties to disgorgement of related profits to criminal fines and sanctions (including imprisonment), depending on the nature and severity of the noncompliance. The penalties for noncompliance can be severe—as high as $800 million in one case.[11]

In today's global economy, it is not uncommon for even relatively small US companies to make sales into, have facilities located in, or otherwise conduct operations in, foreign countries. As such, the opportunity (and temptation) for a US company to actively engage in, or to turn a blind eye

---

[9] 35 U.S.C. § 102 (as amended 2012).
[10] 15 U.S.C. § 78dd-1 *et seq.* (West 1977).
[11] *Foreign Firms Most Affected by a U.S. Law Barring Bribes*, NEW YORK TIMES (September 3, 2012.

to, violations of the FCPA is far greater than was the case at the time of the law's original passage.

Depending on the facts, a buyer may be subject to successor liability for a target company's pre-closing FCPA violations. However, published guidance from the US Department of Justice suggests that buyers that engage in reasonable due diligence, investigate potential FCPA violations, and disclose the same to the government, are less likely to be charged with pre-acquisition violations.[12] Given the increased level of enforcement of the FCPA, the severity of penalties for noncompliance, the greater potential for noncompliance in today's global economy, and the opportunity to reduce or eliminate related exposure through due diligence and remedial action, a thorough due diligence review should include a careful review of the target company's foreign operations, FCPA compliance policies, and related sales and business practices.

*State and Local Tax Liability*

An important area of tax due diligence is state and local tax exposure, which in the past was sometimes overlooked or deemphasized by some buyers. Increasingly, though, buyers are coming to the realization that state and local tax issues can be a major impediment to a deal or can materially negatively impact the value of the target company. For example, a target company's historical after-tax earnings may be inflated due to a failure to properly pay certain state or local taxes. Therefore, it is critical to compare the locations in which the target company conducts business with the states and localities in which it files tax returns.

A concept known as "economic nexus" may result in a company being deemed to be "doing business" in a state based on the amount of its economic activity in that state, including its sales into that state, even if the company does not have a physical location in that state.[13] The flip side of

---

[12] U.S. Dep't of Justice & U.S. Securities & Exchange Commission, Resource Guide to the U.S. Foreign Corrupt Practices Act (2012).
[13] *See, e.g.,* Bloomberg BNA Special Report 2013 Survey of State Tax Departments - Key Findings and Analysis (2013), http://www.bna.com/uploadedFiles/Content/PDFs/2013_Survey_State_Tax_Dept.pdf.

the coin is that state and local tax due diligence may bring to light tax planning opportunities that may enable a buyer to take advantage of tax credits or incentives following the acquisition, thereby increasing the future value of the target business.

*Earnings Sustainability*

It has become increasingly common for buyers to engage an independent accounting firm to conduct a "quality of earnings" or "earnings sustainability" study of the target company as part of the due diligence process. Such a study is different from an audit, both in its purpose and its scope. Some of the factors considered in a quality of earnings analysis are the target company's revenue recognition policies, non-recurring revenues and expenses, unrecorded or under-recorded liabilities, and operational risks that could negatively impact future earnings (e.g., high customer concentration, numerous related party transactions, or excess dependency on a small number of key personnel).

*Patient Protection and Affordable Care Act*

The enactment of the Patient Protection and Affordable Care Act[14] (ACA) in 2010 has increased the level of diligence directed to a target company's employee health benefit plan(s). The length and complexity of the ACA and related regulations (which continue to be promulgated), as well as the many changes to the ACA's requirements and related effective dates that have been announced by the Obama Administration, make such a review a fluid and challenging exercise.

Due diligence with respect to the ACA may entail (i) a review of the number of "full-time" employees of the target company and its affiliates for the purposes of the ACA; (ii) whether such employees are provided the minimum coverage specified in the ACA (or, if not, whether the plan(s) are grandfathered under the Act); (iii) the amount charged to employees for such coverage (calculated as a percentage of each employee's household income); and (iv) the range of potential fees, penalties, and taxes to which the target company may be subject under the ACA.

---

[14] Pub. L. No. 111-148, 124 Stat. 119 (2010).

## Due Diligence in the Current Deal Environment

We currently are experiencing a "sellers' market" in which there are too many qualified buyers chasing too few high-quality deals. As a result, sellers' expectations and their relative leverage have increased. Not surprisingly, this dynamic has resulted in higher EBITDA valuation multiples and purchase prices. It also has resulted in shorter survival periods for sellers' representations and warranties, decreased indemnification obligations for sellers, and lower escrow amounts.[15] Those changes increase the post-closing exposure of buyers, which makes it even more important for buyers to conduct thorough due diligence reviews of target companies before purchasing them.

Buyers of businesses are becoming increasingly sensitive to deal-related costs and expenses. For example, general counsel of public companies often utilize an RFP process to select outside counsel for transactions, and sometimes require reduced fees, a fee cap, or other alternative fee arrangements as a condition to a law firm's engagement.[16] Buyers and their advisors are motivated to reduce transaction costs wherever possible, including by conducting an efficient, focused, and streamlined due diligence process. Unfortunately, at times that cost sensitivity may cause buyers to shortchange the due diligence process, which in turn could result in unnecessary liabilities and exposure for the buyer down the road.

Owners of privately held companies are becoming better educated about the mechanics of selling a business, and the pros and cons of different sale processes. Although "proprietary" sales of private companies to buyers still occur on a regular basis, it is more common for those companies to be sold through an auction process managed by an investment banking firm. Many business owners conclude that such a competitive sale process is more likely to result in the highest possible purchase price and other seller-favorable terms. The vast majority of

---

[15] Mergers & Acquisitions Committee of the American Bar Association Business Law Section, Private Target Mergers & Acquisitions Deal Points Study (Including Transactions Completed in 2012) (2013).

[16] *See, e.g.*, Use of Alternative Fee Arrangements to Pay for Legal Services Heats Up in U.S. (ALM Media Properties) (May 9, 2013).

such auctions employ an online or virtual data room to facilitate the due diligence review of the target company by prospective buyers. Virtual data rooms offer many advantages over physical data rooms, including ease of access, 24/7 availability, discretion/anonymity, and the ability to track each reviewer's activities on the data site. The prevalence of deal auctions and virtual data rooms has facilitated buyers' due diligence reviews of target companies while simultaneously reducing the time and cost of such diligence.

## Conclusion

Due diligence has evolved over the years. Just as boxes of data and physical data rooms have become extinct, the scope and process of due diligence have changed. Information about target companies, their executives, products, and reputation can now be found, at the press of a button, by searching the Internet. As transacting business becomes more "virtual," and as businesses respond to advances in technology, changes in the economy, and new risk management techniques, the issues investigated during the due diligence process will continue to change. The key for practitioners will be to keep up with those changes and appropriately modify due diligence practices to ensure that clients are able to make fully informed investment decisions.

## Key Takeaways

- Due diligence serves many different purposes, including validating the purchase price, verifying the accuracy and completeness of disclosures about the target company, providing specific information that can be used for risk allocation purposes, and identifying the impediments to, and hidden costs of, a transaction.
- Due diligence is an interdisciplinary process, and should be approached in a disciplined, organized manner.
- Investigation of social media relating to the target company has become a common aspect of due diligence, and new online searching tools and recent SEC pronouncements are likely to accelerate that trend.
- Different types of M&A insurance products—including general representation and warranty insurance, and special environmental

and tax insurance—have become increasingly common, and this trend has impacted the timing and manner of due diligence.

- Over the past few years, buyers and their counsel have increased the level of their due diligence in a number of areas, including intellectual property matters, state and local tax issues, earnings sustainability, compliance with the Foreign Corrupt Practices Act, and the potential impact of the Affordable Care Act.

- A number of recent or accelerating trends have affected the manner in which due diligence is conducted, including the leverage that sellers have in today's market, increased sensitivity to deal-related costs for many buyers, and the prevalence of deal auctions and virtual data rooms.

*Jennifer L. Vergilii is a partner at Calfee Halter & Griswold LLP. Her practice focuses on counseling public and privately held clients with respect to a wide range of general corporate and business matters as well as mergers and acquisitions. Ms. Vergilii is actively involved in many start-up ventures, providing legal advice that allows her clients to make sound business decisions. She has extensive experience working with individuals and companies with respect to sales, service, transition and distribution agreements, as well as employment and consulting agreements.*

*Neil J. Whitford, a partner at Calfee Halter & Griswold LLP, represents buyers and sellers of businesses in asset purchases, stock purchases, and mergers. He represents both domestic and international companies, including start-up enterprises, closely held companies, and publicly traded companies. Mr. Whitford assists clients with business formation, private placements, sales and distribution arrangements, employment and consulting agreements, real estate matters, and executive compensation plans.*

# Evolving IP and International Concerns Continually Add New Challenges for M&A Attorneys

Gerard O'Connor

*Partner*

Saul Ewing LLP

ASPATORE

## Introduction

The job of conducting legal "due diligence" in M&A transactions occupies a paradoxical position. It is a task that most often falls to the junior members of the legal team, but legal due diligence is a critical foundation for the legal support of the deal. Recent trends in due diligence practice and issues only serve to emphasize this central role. Due diligence is always becoming more strategic. Buyers are increasingly apprehensive about getting stuck post-closing and finding unexpected liabilities or liabilities for which they were not adequately prepared. For more mature companies, there is a lot more attention than in the past to specialized procedures like quality of earnings and assessment of the targets' backlog.

Also, what constitutes adequate due diligence depends to a great extent on the size and type of transaction. If you represent a private equity firm, then the due diligence process might be driven by the seller's investment banker, who will have established an extensive data room with every conceivable corporate record, or at least this is what it wants to offer up. At the other end of the spectrum, your client might be making a $200,000 aqui-hire of a start-up, its founder, and its single product under development. Toward this end of the spectrum, the buyer's counsel must think strategically and creatively about how to most effectively and efficiently help your client determine that the benefits to the deal are real, and that the risks are manageable. This chapter is intended to apply to deals across the spectrum, but most particularly to those transactions in which counsel plays a more strategic role in framing and executing this critical support role.

## Recent Trends and Issues

- *Financial Due Diligence*: Recently, there has been an increasing or sustained trend toward greater financial due diligence—i.e., review of the target's financial records and operating history—as part of the legal due diligence process. Also, we are seeing a heightened scrutiny of business and financial relationships, particularly where the owners of the target (who are receiving the funds from the transaction) are overseas.

- *Anti-Money Laundering:* Buyers' lawyers need to pay careful attention to where the deal funds are coming from, and where they are going. Anti-money laundering and Patriot Act provisions are increasingly playing a role at the diligence stage. It has become a commonplace closing issue to require various compliance documentation from owners of the selling or buying company when the funds are coming from overseas. This results in a delay with getting everything squared away. That process is better addressed in the due diligence stage, now that M&A practitioners have become more accustomed to these heightened financial reporting requirements.

- *Investment from Foreign Jurisdictions:* We are also seeing an increase in foreign money coming over to US companies in early stage investment as well as in M&A. In a straight domestic deal where there is no foreign money, the financial due diligence is comparatively easier. But in an M&A transaction involving foreign buyers, you need to track the money, ensure appropriate tax reporting and withholding, and make sure that all parties comply with anti-money laundering laws. This includes, when necessary, retaining local counsel to ensure compliance with local laws of other jurisdictions. Awareness of potential international issues in due diligence is going to continue to be more important. For the early stage companies that make up my own tech M&A practice, the population of companies available for acquisition is increasingly multinational from day one. My own recent clients have included Delaware corporations with operations in Turkey, Columbia, India, and North Africa, as well as Western Europe. There is a lot going on at the early stage across multiple jurisdictions, and that makes the due diligence process much more complex if someone wants to buy one of these companies. M&A attorneys who can get their arms around how to effectively conceive of, strategize around, and carry out a diligence process for a small M&A target with complex multinational operations and different people from different places making up the management team are going to work more effectively than their counterparts who are comparatively less familiar prepared attorneys accustomed to using a standard due diligence document request list and—if you have a buyer or seller from another country—calling in a local law firm to duplicate the process in the other jurisdiction. M&A attorneys from different jurisdictions are going to have to nimbly and effectively work together to do proper due diligence cost effectively without overwhelming the deal with legal fees that cannot be justified.

- *Customers*: Visits to customers and the customer-based due diligence increasingly happening earlier in the process, and the conditions of customer interviews and visits, are more likely to be negotiated at the term-sheet stage, as opposed to later in the process as issues come up. Sellers do not tend to like buyers going to their customers until the very end of the process, if at all. However, buyers are increasingly pushing for access to that type of due diligence earlier in the process.

- *Employee Benefits*: A thorough due diligence effort needs to include a review of employee retirement plans. This area is highly technical, and in recent years various provisions of the federal ERISA statute have required plans to amend their terms. It is quite common to encounter instances of noncompliance in this area, particularly when the target is a smaller, privately held company.

- *Data Rooms*: Throughout the range of deal size, the data room is definitely here to stay as a crucial due diligence tool. The days of shipping documents to people are long over. The data room is more than a convenient place to put documents, though. It should also be used strategically. The seller team can use the data room to monitor who is in the data room and what documents or categories they are viewing.

- *Data Compliance and Privacy Issues*: This category is driven equally by new substantive law as well as by good old fear of the unknown. Lawyers who have been practicing this area for a while may remember back when, for a brief period of time, Y2K compliance and related issues were a big deal. Every deal included a full-fledged fore drill on the target's "Y2K readiness" and gallons of ink were spent on writing up reps and warranties about Y2K, in case all of the computers stopped working on January 1, 2000. That turned out to be a tempest in a teapot. Today, data collection, preservation and privacy concerns are going to be issues that remain high priorities for the foreseeable future. In any kind of technology company, the history of the company's compliance with various data management and privacy laws is becoming increasingly important. This is with good reason, but also, this is an area in which lawyers can get carried away. You should make sure that your due diligence strategy on data issues addresses the legitimate risks posed by the parties' businesses and use of data.

## Effective Due Diligence Strategies

The first key component of an effective due diligence strategy includes making sure that the right people on the team are conducting due diligence. Sometimes, due diligence seems to be conducted upside down. The most junior members of the legal and financial teams are assigned to "do the due diligence," and it is carried out as more of a preordained set of steps: draft the document request list (using a form list from the last few deals) and get a pile of documents, review them, and write a memo analyzing the relevant points and issues. In fact, the most effective due diligence process starts at the highest level. Using precedent forms for document requests and other precedent forms is certainly helpful for a general framework, but it is also important to talk to the buyer's principals about the biggest business risks they see with respect to the target company.

Likewise, the documents that the seller chooses to put in the data room may omit some categories or documents that are important to the buyer. To make this determination you need to think about the client's objectives. What are they trying to accomplish by making the acquisition? What might prevent them? It is important to bring senior legal and financial resources to bear in assessing the likely risks post-closing, and then thinking strategically about how to turn that into a request for interviews, information, or data from the seller.

What follows is the process of making sure the information is reviewed in the right way by the right people at the right time. Ensuring the right senior strategic focus and guidance in the diligence process is what separates effective and efficient diligence processes from diligence processes that slow down deals and produce a lot of paper and memos.

Every deal is different, and of course, the issue you did not pay enough attention to is the one that inevitably erupts the day before closing. Differences also depend on the industry and the size of the deal. Common "repeat offenders" include:

- Contracts: What happens to certain contracts of the seller—i.e., can they be assigned, is someone's consent needed, and what happens if you do not get consent? What about contracts that are ambiguous—e.g., that do not specifically speak to the effect of the precise type of deal that is happening?

- Creditors: Are there parties who either need to be paid off or need to be behind the new owners in terms of subordinating security interests or taking junior rights to payment back? Attention needs to be paid to them.

- Employees: This might be the most commonly mismanaged element of the due diligence process. Often, the buyer wants to make sure it gets the services of the critical employees of the seller going forward. That expectation will be stated in a term sheet as a condition to the deal and it will be put into the purchase agreement as a condition of the deal, but it might not be pursued as energetically or as early on as a diligence matter. There are many reasons for this. The employees are not necessarily involved in the day-to-day negotiation and diligence process. Sometimes, the seller does not want employees even to know that negotiations for the sale of the company are taking place. Anyway, crucial questions can get lost in the shuffle, such as: do these people want to come and work for the buyer? Do negotiations have to take place? Do the critical employees have benefits packages in place that might not fit with the buyer's policies and procedures? Are they going to feel like they are being courted by someone who values their contributions to the seller and the buyer in the future? Or are they going to feel like, at the last minute, someone shoved an employment agreement into their hand and said, "Sign this by tomorrow or we cannot close"? That is a risk that cuts across deals of all sizes in all industries. One must make sure that the proper attention is paid to the employees of the seller who are important to the buyer. Often, that is lost in the rush. Sometimes those very important people are pushed to the side until the very end of the process, and that is not a good way to establish a relationship. Make sure consideration of employee issues is part of the critical due diligence process.

## Developing or Updating a Diligence Strategy

When developing a diligence strategy for a buyer, start with the top reasons the buyer wants to buy this company. What is the acquisition going to do for the buyer? What are the three to five best things the buyer sees happening if it closes the deal? After you make that list, then find out about the three to five things the buyer is most afraid of happening if it buys this company. Then, the things that the buyer is most worried about happening if it does not buy this company. Will a competitor buy it? For an attorney on the buyer side, it is important to start with just listening to the client. You must find out what your client is most interested in, and motivated by. That way, in the due diligence process, you can make sure those good things are really there; you can also investigate the threat posed by the most worrisome things, and determine whether those things seem like real risks. The standard-issue due diligence document request is fine, but if you start from a prescriptive list then you might miss out on understanding the top drivers or risks for your client. Instead, start with what the client wants to do, why the client wants to do it, and a little bit of that background. Then, go to the list and look at it with a view toward whether it is going to flesh out whether the good things the clients wants are there and measure whether the bad things the client fears are there. Then I either start over or modify the document request list.

## Role of M&A Attorneys During Phases of Due Diligence

*Seller Side*

On the seller's side, if your client is using a banker, then you should review any "teasers" or sales documents before they are used. You want to make sure that nothing in it is getting off on the wrong foot. These are generally considered by the deal team to be "sales documents, not liability documents," and so sometimes extensive legal review is discouraged. After all, the definitive merger or purchase agreement will contain the extensively negotiated representations and warranties, and limitations, and will contain an "integration clause" stating that it is the "entire agreement" between the parties. However, you should make sure your clients realize that this so-called "integration clause" in the definitive agreement will not necessarily absolve the seller of liability for other alleged misrepresentations. The Massachusetts Supreme Judicial Court, for example, has held that an integration clause is not enough to dismiss a claim alleging violations of state securities laws in prior communications between the parties.[1] Therefore, you need to make sure that *all* material disclosures are accurate, and not just the ones in the "entire agreement."

The target company's attorney hopefully will have been hard at work for a long time before that disclosure is requested, because it takes a while to prepare and figure out what kind of data room to establish, and the right way to format and organize documents. It can take a long time to make sure it is complete and accurate. The target company's M&A attorney should be working with investment bankers or other consultants early in the process, to help the company anticipate and fix diligence issues. This work may include, for example, negotiating a new agreement or extending an existing agreement with a key customer, looking back and ensuring all employees have made the appropriate assignments of intellectual

---

[1] *See Marram v. Kobrick Offshore Fund, Ltd.*, 442 Mass. 43 (2004).

property, or reviewing a lease to, for example, ensure a sufficient number of extension options to satisfy the buyer's need for certainty (especially for retail, medical/dental or other location dependent companies). Work for M&A attorneys on the sell side starts long before the non-disclosure agreement is signed.

*Buyer Side*

For the buyer side, attorneys want to make sure that they are driving the process. Do not necessarily accept the seller's invitation: "Here is the data room, go look at it, everything is there." That may or may not satisfy you—if you have had your strategic due diligence meeting with the high-level executives from the buyer, you may have other questions. You may have customers you want to talk to. You may have more questions about the seller's technology. You may have senior employees at the seller that you want to interview. There may be a lot of tasks on your due diligence list of concerns that are not adequately addressed by the seller's pre-established data room, and you should take the opportunity to get some control over the process after the NDA is signed.

*Accounting and Legal Due Diligence*

You generally do not wind up adding much value by having a lot of lawyers looking at accounting due diligence—or visa versa—but the M&A attorney on the buy side can add value to his or her client by ensuring that the accountants are reviewing the accounting due diligence and identifying the issues in a way that is meaningful to the legal process. At the end of the day, the M&A process is a legal process. Finding accounting issues is great, but only if that finding turns into a provision in the document that appropriately allocates the risk of that accounting issue. Often we say, "I am going to look at the legal documents, and the accountants look at the accounting documents," but you have to make sure that the two teams are communicating at a meaningful level so that legitimate accounting issues are captured and weighed within the legal risk allocation process, and also so that, conversely, accounting issues that may not be material or that are easily resolved do not unnecessarily sidetrack the parties. Sometimes another advisor might be doing financial due diligence that is separate from the accounting due diligence—i.e., quality of earnings review. The M&A attorney has to be the quarterback of the team, making sure that any issues revealed (whether in review of accounting procedures of the company, in the quality of earnings review, or in legal due diligence to the extent that they constitute risk for the buyer) are appropriately communicated among the team and handled in the deal documents.

## Handling Non-Public Information

Typically, a non-disclosure agreement or NDA is one of the first documents to be signed in an M&A process, before any meaningful due diligence takes place. Almost everything that the seller provides is confidential from the seller's perspective. The last thing the seller wants is to show the prospective buyer a potential market opportunity or a confidential customer list, and then have the buyer take advantage of that outside of the M&A process. That is critical, and the NDA is important. However, the business ethics of the parties to the transaction are just as important, because once the information is made available, it can be difficult to prevent an unscrupulous party from misusing it. Dealing with the right people and advisors and establishing a level of trust early on is at least as critical as the language in the NDA.

### Before the NDA Is Signed

Seller teams should, of course, respond cautiously to requests for non-public information before the NDA is signed. If you do not have an NDA, you might as well leave your confidential information at the nearest Starbucks. Many deals start with executive-to-executive discussions on a somewhat casual basis, and with initial disclosure of information with the understanding that it is confidential. The lawyers are brought in if there is enough joint interest in proceeding to construct the framework of an actual deal. I tend to take a fairly dim view of too much sharing of public information before an NDA is in place. It goes without saying that for public companies, even the fact that discussions are taking place can put the parties and their advisors in the reach of insider trading regulations. Even for a private company, exchange of confidential information can lead to antitrust concerns if it is not managed properly. Also, you may lose rights to patent your technology if you disclose it on a non-confidential basis, and you may lose trade secrets if you disclose them without securing appropriate protection against the recipient's further use or disclosure. I would be leery of sharing too much information casually or before an NDA is signed. Any pre-NDA disclosure should be done cautiously and with the benefit of legal advice and review.

*After the NDA Is Drafted*

After the NDA is drafted, the position of the buyer is now, "I am going to spend time and money, so I want an open window into this company." That is fine. But on the other hand, simply because an NDA is in place does not mean that the seller's problems are all solved. In negotiating the NDA, the seller should be careful to address things like (i) who are the specific people who are to be allowed access to the confidential information and (ii) what are the protocols around handling, copying, incorporating into buyer-generated property like due diligence memoranda, and disposing of, the information. In any case, after the NDA is in place, if there is a data room, then the buyer's designated individuals should get access to it. If there is no data room, then the parties might bring the buyer's advisors in to view documents at the target, or send documents to the buyer, or establish a data room *ad hoc*. Some specific issues with respect to post-NDA diligence matters include:

- Unpublished Patent Applications and File Histories: Provisional patent applications, as well as unpublished patent applications and file histories, may be requested by the intellectual property practitioners on the acquiring company for review. Some care should be taken here, especially if the target and buyer are competitors in an IP-dominated field such as pharmaceuticals.

As a first measure, maybe the seller can offer a seller counsel-prepared analysis. Generally, the first analysis should be by qualified counsel outside of the acquiring company, subject to a conflict check to make sure that the individual attorneys reviewing the materials are not closely involved in similar work and at some point—when the deal gets more mature—the appropriate IP people at the company should look at it. If the deal goes south and does not close, you want to avoid the possibility of the seller complaining later that the IP has been misappropriated. I would do a first pass through legal and let a qualified patent attorney comment on the quality of the patent application and file histories and office actions.

- Future Marketing Plans: The seller's future marketing plans fall into the category of things that the seller really may or may not want to share. The seller may be very touchy about what the buyer is going to do with these plans. At the same time, the right people within the buyer probably need to look at them. Actually, sometimes the seller's future marketing plans are material to the buyer, and in other cases they are not. Instagram's future marketing plans were probably not the least bit important to Facebook. However, if a private equity firm is buying a product manufacturing company, the future marketing plans might be critical. If the seller is a strategic buyer that is a competitor of the seller, maybe the seller's future marketing plans probably warrant more cautious treatment. If the buyer is a private equity company or other financial buyer, that concern is typically more attenuated, unless the private equity company is also a potential investor in competitors.

## Dealing with Information Sought and Found in Due Diligence

As the deal attorney, you will be the one making the analysis of the information, and you are looking for indicators of risk. Typically, by the time you are at the legal due diligence stage, you probably know your buyer client's good reasons to make the acquisition. It might be accretive to buyer's financial performance; it might supply the buyer with critical user base; or it might add a piece of critical functionality to the buyer's technology. So you know why you want to do the deal, and you probably have a price tag, deal structure, and some expectations as to how the deal is going to look on the closing date. In due diligence, you are essentially looking for reasons why not to do the deal, at least not on the economic terms set forth in the term sheet. By the time you are at diligence, you probably have a price tag, deal structure, and some expectations as to how the deal is going to look on the closing date.

In diligence, if you come across risk then identify it, assess it, and communicate it. Then the question becomes: can the parties allocate this newly discovered risk within the deal that is already struck, such that the deal can continue? If, for example, you come across a whopping potential tax liability because the seller has been in violation of ERISA with respect to its retirement plans, then maybe not. That might be significant enough to either force a revaluation of the company, especially for a smaller deal, or maybe you can put some money in escrow, make a corrective filing, and let that process play out post-closing. Whether it is tax, accounting, employment, IP, or the many other categories of due diligence, you are really looking to identify previously undisclosed risk and, once you find it, try to allocate it within the structure of the deal.

The type of information found during the diligence process really depends on the type and size of the company. For a while, it seemed like I was not doing any deal where I did not find some sort of ERISA compliance issue. These days, we are finding banking or data privacy issues. The issues that commonly come up in due diligence, to the extent they can be categorized, tend to be matters that are complex, technical, and new enough so that particularly small target companies lack the bandwidth or expertise to have mastered them. Typically, the larger companies buying them do have the bandwidth, within the company or in the ranks of their professional advisors, to know enough to be on the lookout for these issues. If there have been amendments to laws in the recent past, then larger, more sophisticated companies may be aware of where missteps may be taking place, whereas smaller, and perhaps less well-funded, companies may not be able to keep up. These issues can involve things like benefits plans, anti-money laundering statutes, privacy, and data protection.

**Special Issues for Tech Start-Ups**

Early stage, fast-growing technology companies can face special due diligence risks. The technology process is insufficient in terms of number and quality of IP assignments by founders and employees. If the buyer does not feel like all of the people who have contributed to the intellectual property of the target have made valid assignments, then that will be a problem and it will hold up the deal until any "missing" assignments are accounted for. If your client's company was started at a weekend hackathon, how do you make sure that you have all of the inventors' names on the patent application? Also, in a fast-moving tech start-up, "forgotten founders" come out of the woodwork at the most inconvenient times—i.e., when they get wind of the deal, making claims to equity of the target. Or maybe the target was a little too casual in issuing equity to its founders and advisors—"5 percent of the company" on the date of incorporation is a lot different from 5 percent after a significant investment.

Sometimes, early stage technology companies feel like their potential suitors are really just trying to get a free look at the company's technology under the guise of negotiating a *bona fide* transaction. As an M&A attorney who has seen a lot of deal processes, some of which do seem to fall into this category, I suggest having a basically trusting view of the world, along with a healthy dose of skepticism. Sometimes the acquirer or would-be acquirer is on a fishing expedition. Being careful to engage in the process in a deliberate way is important. It does not happen as often as some of the more paranoid of my early stage clients think it happens, but fishing for information definitely happens. Clients who are concerned about this trick should take the time to sound people out. Talk about the nature of their interest, what they see happening in a combination or other agreement, what they want to do that they cannot currently do and how you can help them. Listen to the answers and, if they sound plausible, then you should maybe risk moving forward. If it sounds like they just want a lot of information and to kick the tires, then proceed cautiously.

## Advice for Junior M&A Attorneys

Attorneys new to the mergers and acquisition field should find an experienced firm or a team to work with. Get in on all the deals possible. Remember that often when you are the junior attorney burning the midnight oil looking over the list of contracts, you might be the one who saves or kills the deal. Unlike many junior-level assignments, due diligence stands out because it is something a junior attorney does that can be extremely critical to the client's success, whether the deal goes forward or not. Often, it is that junior associate who first identifies the issue that then gets flagged for the senior members of the team. Finding the right team, getting on the right deals, and taking ownership of the process by flagging things that look wrong are good ways to get ahead. You have an enormous job to digest a lot of information, prioritize issues, and make sure they are attended to by the team that may be drafting the document or negotiating the financial terms of the deal. You play a critical role. Interact with the senior lawyers on your team and be aware of your critical role.

## Conclusion

As a start-up lawyer, I am always thinking about due diligence issues that the company will face in its eventual exit or liquidity transaction. Sometimes, when I am advising a start-up client, we find ourselves discussing whether a particular point in a negotiation is important or not. For example, a cross party to an NDA might be asking for an unusual change to the standard definition of "confidential information." Or, a member of the founding team might be balking at signing the company's standard intellectual property assignment. I often find myself advising the client that, while the point in contention might not be important for the immediate purpose of the negotiation, we are also building a due diligence record for the eventual investor in, or acquiror of, our company, and that the overall posture of the company at that time might be affected by decisions we make now. The point is "due diligence" is always happening. The record of the company's activities that make up the due diligence file, which will eventually be reviewed by a potential acquirer, is constantly being created with every action and decision you and your client take from the date of inception. As the world of technology start-ups becomes more and more complex and global, the lawyers that act as general counsel and M&A counsel to these entities must develop a sophisticated, but right-sized, approach to creating, curating, and presenting to interested parties the due diligence record of your client company, and they must develop and exercise an increasingly sophisticated understanding of the lawyer's role in this process.

**Key Takeaways**

- Put some senior legal and financial resources to bear in assessing the likely risks post-closing, then be strategic about how to turn that into a request for interviews, information or data from the seller.

- Be aware of all international aspects of your client's business. Is intellectual property being developed internationally? Will operations take place in other countries?

- Make sure the employees are considered part of the critical due diligence process. One of the most important aspects of diligence is retaining the services of the critical employees of the seller going forward.

- Dealing with the right people and advisors and establishing a level of trust early on is more critical than the words on the NDA.

- When updating or developing a diligence strategy for a buyer as an M&A attorney, start with the top reasons the buyer wants to buy the company and the top risks the buyer anticipates.

- Make sure you are involved in review of all disclosures, not just the ones in the definitive documents.

- If you represent start-ups and early stage technology companies, remember that you are always creating your client's due diligence record, which will be scrutinized before the client successfully exits.

- Most importantly, do not be timid about raising issues and asking questions just because you happen to be the most junior person on the deal.

*Gerard O'Connor is a partner at Saul Ewing LLP. Mr. O'Connor's practice focuses on business matters ranging from mergers and acquisitions and corporate finance to intellectual property. He represents clients in a variety of industries including clean energy technology, renewable energy, software and information technology, manufacturing, venture capital, and professional services.*

# We Disclosed What? Seller Strategies to Mitigate Risks Associated with Evolving Information Evaluation Techniques

James A. Butz

*Member*

Frost Brown Todd LLC

ASPATORE

## Introduction

The resources available and techniques used by buyers to obtain, extract, and evaluate due diligence information continue to evolve. In response, sellers need to be mindful of including appropriate disclaimers that accompany the information when disclosed, and when and how the information will be disclosed, and including "anti-sandbagging" language in definitive documents. Failure to do so may result in a post-closing claim for indemnification asserted by a buyer against a seller for a breach of a representation and warranty, even though the seller may be unaware of the results of the buyer's evaluation.

## Evolving Due Diligence Practices

Preliminary discussions involving non-confidential information have taken place, and buyer and seller have executed a confidentiality agreement. There seems to be common ground for the basis of a transaction so buyer and seller then execute a letter of intent. Next, seller may receive a request[1] containing language similar to the following:

> In connection with the acquisition of seller, please provide us with the following materials. If certain materials have already been provided or are unavailable, please indicate so in your response. Our due diligence investigation is ongoing and we will submit supplemental due diligence requests as necessary.

- All contracts with customers or suppliers
- Complete list of customers for the last three years indicating dollar amounts and nature of services provided
- Complete list of current suppliers indicating dollar amounts and nature of products supplied

---

[1] A typical due diligence request would of course be much more detailed and contain comprehensive requests for information covering a variety of topics.

- Pertinent market research or marketing studies (including any studies or reports relied on or commissioned or prepared by seller)
- Any recent analyses of seller prepared by investment bankers, engineers, management consultants, auditors or others
- Recent presentations to industry, trade or investment groups
- Marketing and sales literature and forms, including price lists, catalogs, purchase orders, technical manuals, and user manuals
- All financial statements with accompanying management reports and policies

Seller makes such information available[2] and, as the due diligence process progresses, buyer then requests to contact seller's customers and suppliers for the purpose of extracting additional information (such as customer loyalty or supplier commitment to pricing stability) which will be analyzed, in detail, to predict future revenue streams. When such revenue streams are not realized post-closing, buyer then asserts a claim against seller. How should have the seller responded?

Buyers have employed increasingly sophisticated techniques in recent times to not only assess the existing risks associated with the acquisition of a business, but also to evaluate and predict the driving factors associated with most acquisitions—i.e., future revenue realization. For example, a buyer may engage business-to-business research companies to gain valuable intelligence about a seller's customers, such as an understanding of a particular customer's needs and perspective. Research companies use predictive analytics to retain and enhance customer relationships. For example, through customer surveying, a research company with oftentimes exacting precision can predict that 10 percent of seller's customers have no loyalty and would change suppliers if given any reasonable opportunity, 20 percent of the seller's customers

---

[2] Seller may make information available through delivery of documents or more frequently through access to a virtual data room.

are extremely loyal and, absent a significant event, would not change suppliers, and the remaining 70 percent of the customers are likely to remain customers but are vigilant to opportunities to change or modify an arrangement (especially if the change involves the price of the product). In addition, research companies can identify opportunities to expand product lines, introduce new product lines or increase price.

Because of the increased emphasis on profitability, a conservative lending environment, and the historically high failure (inability to achieve profit projections) rate of merger and acquisition transactions, buyers have searched for and utilized techniques to enhance the probability of success. In response to these more invasive techniques, which clearly shift the risk of the success or failure of the transaction, sellers have responded by attempting to limit exposure to post-closing claims based on the due diligence techniques and results of the application of these techniques.

These trends have arisen through the natural evolution of data mining techniques and predictive analysis. However, sellers may not even be aware that such techniques exist or, if sellers are aware of the techniques, they may not understand the purpose and use of such techniques. Almost universally however, sellers do understand and are reluctant to create, either directly or indirectly, a buyer's expectation post-closing as to the operation of the business.

## Responses to Evolving Due Diligence Methods

In response to these evolving due diligence methods, sellers have reacted in a variety of ways, including adding more robust disclaimers to accompany due diligence information, limiting or delaying access to customers and information, and utilizing carefully crafted "anti-sandbagging" information.

*Disclaimers*

An effective method to decrease seller's risk is the use of a disclaimer. A typical disclaimer may state:[3]

---

[3] There are many variations of disclaimer language and because of the precise language

Buyer acknowledges and agrees that neither seller nor any of seller's representatives is making or has made any representation or warranty, express or implied, as to the accuracy or completeness of the information provided by or prepared for seller. Buyer has not and will not rely on any information in connection with buyer's decision to complete this transaction. Neither seller nor any of seller's representatives will have any liability to buyer resulting from buyer's use of the information including buyer's use of raw data to compile predictive reports or information.

This disclaimer would be used before any information is disclosed and several points are critical to effective use. To be effective, the disclaimer must contain some type of buyer reliance component. Otherwise, a savvy buyer will take the position that even though it did indeed agree that the information may not have been complete, buyer relied on the information that was provided, however incomplete. And, even with the buyer reliance component, it is extremely unlikely that the use of any disclaimer would prevent a successful claim by buyer in the event of fraud.[4]

There may be some question regarding the effectiveness of disclaimers given that the definitive document most likely will contain an integration clause. An integration clause integrates all previous negotiations and terms into the definitive document, indicating a final agreement on terms and provisions. Including this provision expresses buyer and seller intention that the definitive document reflects the entire agreement and courts should exclude evidence outside of the definitive document itself if a dispute arises. So does this mean that the disclaimer will be useless once the definitive documents are executed? Not necessarily. Any post-closing claim asserted by a buyer likely will include fraud claims and, with such claims, courts have generally gone beyond the definitive documents to accept evidence. Once a

---

may be the subject of intense negotiation between buyer and seller.
[4] *See*, for example, *Transdigm Inc. v. Alcoa Global Fasteners, Inc.*, CIV.A. 7135-VCP, 2013 WL 2326881 (Del. Ch. May 29, 2013). *Compare, Universal Enter. Grp., L.P. v. Duncan Petroleum Corp.*, CV 4948-VCL, 2013 WL 3353743 (Del. Ch. July 1, 2013).

court is willing to do so, a disclaimer may properly be admitted as evidence, especially in the absence of a non-reliance clause.

*Limiting or Controlling Access*

Another seller response to buyers' request is to carefully control when and how information is disclosed or made available. Typically, a letter of intent will contain contingencies[5] to the obligation of buyer to proceed with the transaction. Sellers will disclose generic information but tend to delay sensitive information such as pricing and customer lists until the transaction matures and the contingencies are removed. Direct contact with customers may never be allowed but that is often a function of the relative leverage of the parties. Research companies may entice sellers to allow access, reasoning that even if the transaction does not go forward the information gained will be valuable to seller going forward. So, in response to buyer's request to access customers directly (which may be through email surveys, telephone calls or, less often, direct visits), seller may simply say "no," or allow access but carefully monitor it. In any event, seller needs to actively participate and manage customer contact to reduce the risk of misinterpreted information resulting from the survey process.

*Use of Anti-Sandbagging Provisions*

During the transaction, seller and buyer will work toward the completion of a definitive document (such as an asset purchase agreement). The definitive document will contain seller representations[6] relating to the status of customer relationships and changes in the business prospects. An astute seller will certainly envision a situation where buyer learns new information during customer due diligence, fails to disclose such adverse material information to seller, closes the transaction, and then seeks a damage claim against seller for breach of a representation and warranty. Seller's method to avoid such a claim is to include an "anti-sandbagging" provision in the definitive document. A typical provision is as follows:

---

[5] Contingences include completion of due diligence investigation, obtaining satisfactory financing and obtaining board and shareholder approval.
[6] *See* Appendix A

> Seller shall not be liable under this Agreement for any losses based upon or arising out of any inaccuracy in or breach of any of the representations or warranties of Seller contained in this Agreement if Buyer knows or should have known of such inaccuracy or breach prior to the Closing. Buyer shall be deemed to have waived any breach of any of Seller's representations and warranties and any covenants and agreements of which Buyer has awareness at the closing.

Including this provision in the definitive document will mitigate the risk that buyers conduct predictive analysis, learn of information that constitutes a breach of a representation or warranty, fail to disclose such information to seller, and then pursue seller post-closing for damages for a breach of a representation and warranty.

**Conclusion**

It is clear that as data mining techniques are further refined, and new techniques become available, buyers will use such techniques to probe further to predict the likelihood of the success of a transaction. Sellers will naturally resist the disclosure of this information until such techniques become the custom and sellers understand such techniques and can evaluate the risks. The challenges buyers face include understanding the application of these more predictive analytical techniques. Sellers face the challenge of not being held responsible for the compilation or interpretation of the results of these techniques.

Counsel representing sellers must become familiar with evolving techniques and be able to critically analyze the risks (both legal and business) to properly advise sellers. Counsel should seek third-party assistance as an aid in understanding these techniques. Common responses to evolving due diligence techniques include liberal use of disclaimers, controlling the timing and amount of information disclosed or made available, and including "anti-sandbagging" provisions in definitive documents.

## Key Takeaways

- The beginning of transactions typically move quickly so counsel representing sellers should discuss early with sellers what information will be disclosed, and how and when the information will be disclosed.

- Counsel for sellers should have available appropriate disclaimer language that will need to be included with delivery of materials or as a condition of access to a virtual data room. A review of case law to become familiar with the nuances and interpretations of disclaimers will be invaluable.

- Counsel for buyers should become familiar with new evaluation techniques and share that information with buyers to not only assess the risks associated with the acquisition of a business, but also to evaluate and predict the driving factors associated with most acquisitions—i.e., future revenue realization.

- Counsel for buyers and sellers need to be mindful of the interplay between disclaimers, integration clauses, and anti-sandbagging clauses when beginning the due diligence process and completing definitive documents.

*James A. Butz is a member of Frost Brown Todd LLC where he advises business leaders who invest in growth and build businesses in a variety of transactions, such as mergers and acquisitions, securities offerings, and commercial financings. With over twenty-five years of experience, Mr. Butz has advised business leaders in a number of industries including manufacturing, real estate, information technology, financial services, and health care.*

*Mr. Butz earned his bachelor of science degree from Indiana University where he majored in accounting at Kelley School of Business and received his juris doctor degree from Case Western Reserve School of Law where he served as a staff member of the* Journal of International Law.

# Ten Impediments to a Successful Due Diligence Process and Key Trends Impacting Today's M&A Deals

Michael G. Platner and
Solomon B. Zoberman

*Partners*
Lewis Brisbois Bisgaard & Smith LLP

ASPATORE

## Introduction

In our practice, we are regularly called upon to help clients prepare for and execute due diligence (DD) strategies in connection with various financing or M&A transactions involving privately held companies. The DD process and issues attendant to public companies can be very different from those encountered in private company transactions, largely due to the federal securities laws and concomitant public company reporting requirements. This chapter will focus on DD issues encountered in transactions involving the buying, selling or financing of private companies, or divisions of public companies in circumstances where the DD focus is on information not readily available to the public.

We will discuss what we have over the years observed to be ten of the most significant impediments to a successful DD process, and important things parties can do to better facilitate an efficient and more cost-effective DD process. We will also discuss recent developments and trends in DD.

### Ten Key Impediments to a Successful Due Diligence Review

*1) Be Prepared! Seller's Pre-Process Internal Evaluation and Due Diligence Review*

The first and in our view, foremost, impediment to a successful DD process is the seller's lack of internal protocols with respect to record keeping, document management, intellectual property rights management and the like, coupled with a lack of understanding of what the transaction process in general, and the DD process in particular, will involve.

A seller that knows early on what to expect from the DD process will be more likely to have enough time to accurately identify the relevant records it has (e.g., minutes/consents regarding governance, vendor, supplier and customer contracts, inbound/outbound IP licenses, financial, etc.), those records it is missing and needs, and to organize, index, and review those records in anticipation of the DD process. Careful preparation can and often does surface potentially serious issues before they can be used by a prospective lender or buyer to the seller's disadvantage.

For example, a seller may, upon review of its employment contracts and independent contractor agreements, discover that key intellectual property assets, which it assumed it owned "free and clear," are in fact subject to third-party claims, licenses or rights that would be unacceptable to a lender or purchaser, and which could result in unfavorable terms (e.g. discounted sale price, escrows, etc.), or derail the transaction entirely. Identifying issues during internal pre-process due diligence enables the seller to remedy problems (e.g., effect necessary rights clearance) before commencement of the buyer's due diligence. Such preparation will not only be of benefit to the seller going forward in any event, but also makes it more likely that seller will be able to efficiently and successfully navigate the DD process. Sellers who fail to timely undertake such internal review can find themselves in the position of having to respond to potentially pointed and embarrassing DD inquiries from its banker or a potential buyer, or worse yet, suffer a reduction in selling price, less favorable terms, or lose the deal. This type of internal evaluation should occur before engagement of a banker or marketing of the seller begins.

The pre-process preparation will enable the seller to reasonably anticipate buyer's due diligence requests, and facilitate organization and efficient population of the digital data room.

During this process, seller should identify and also designate the team responsible for coordination and management of the seller side DD process, those people in seller's organization who will be "in the loop," and the point person or designated contact(s) for communications between seller on the one hand, and seller's outside legal counsel, the investment banker or potential buyer(s) on the other hand, as well as concomitant separate confidentiality protocols.

Digital Data Repositories

If the seller has not already done so as a matter of its regular practice, it should set up a digital data repository and formulate its approach and timeframe for gathering and digitizing the records it anticipates will be the subject of DD requests, and transfer that digital information into that repository. Use of digital data repositories in middle market due diligence has been steadily increasing. Many companies have already digitized much of their records and are accustomed to using simple offline cloud storage environments to keep or share files. Because the seller will likely be dealing with a lot of additional information during the DD process, and additional protections will likely be needed for materials that contain or constitute trade secrets or confidential business information, we recommend that sellers start from scratch when it comes to designing the digital data room it will use in the DD process. While corporate management has become increasingly familiar, and comfortable, with the concept of virtual data rooms and there is a lot more marketing by various data room SaaS vendors than in years past, it is important that in preparing for a transaction, sellers pay close attention to vetting and selection of the appropriate digital data room service. Competent data room SaaS vendors enable the smooth transition of data from the seller's own digital database to the virtual data room, where seller should be readily able through use of an intuitive, user friendly interface to restrict access to and track uploads and downloads of its information during the entire DD and transaction process.

Gathering and Organizing Information

It is important that the seller's team leader cause seller's team to gather the necessary DD materials in a timely manner and input them into the protected digital data room environment in a manner that properly distinguishes among and restricts access to categories of materials by level of confidentiality. For example, customer lists or information bearing on research and development or pricing strategies might be ranked at a high level of confidentiality with access restricted to specifically identified individuals and with no permissions granted for downloading or printing of copies. Alternatively, only redacted copies of sensitive information may be loaded to the data room and/or the data room index might indicate that items identified, but not posted, may be viewed by specific personnel upon request, and possibly subject to execution of a separate NDA. On the other hand, data regarding the status of accounts, regular vendors or supplier contracts, assignments of IP rights or internal company governance documents might not warrant the same level of protection.

Problems can occur in situations where a company fails to upload all of its material documents to the virtual data room at the beginning of the DD process and instead adds material from time to time either in a piecemeal fashion or in response to buyer's DD questions. When this happens, questions may be raised by the buyer's team regarding why those documents were not included in the data room to begin with—especially if uploading of new, and material, information occurs after the due diligence process is well underway. This not only can be distracting, but also can communicate a lack of appropriate decision making by the seller, or worse yet, call into question seller's ability to completely comply, or to comply in good faith, with the buyer's DD requests.

Again, it is important for the seller to have conducted its own thorough, internal pre-process due diligence review. To ensure that it has gathered all relevant records and identified potential issues that might, if left unaddressed, cause the potential buyer to question the value of the seller's business, form the basis for buyer to seek a discount of the purchase price, insist on an earn-out or escrow not previously contemplated in the LOI, or call into question seller's good faith. Sometimes the seller is surprised to learn how much time is being taken up by the internal pre-DD evaluation process. Most companies do not have highly qualified personnel with an extra forty hours a week to spare over a period of three or four weeks to engage in all of the necessary data gathering, transitioning, uploading, indexing, and answering of questions. Limiting the number of people who are involved in the pre-diligence review process is a key part of preparation. It is not only sufficient to be prepared in the abstract, it is critical for a company to assign a few leaders who will be responsible for making the internal pre-process review and the subsequent DD process go smoothly.

*2) Assigning Accountability for Key Issues*

Another impediment to a successful DD process is failure to clearly identify who on the seller's team will be ultimately accountable for deliverables or completing particular action items. For example, responses to accounting due diligence questions may rest with the CFO, outside accountants, or with other persons important to the process. It is critical that one "quarterback" be designated to keep the respective team members on task and on schedule, to make sure that information is available when called for—and that questions are answered timely by the appropriate seller representative.

Where a seller takes great pains, at significant expense, to gather and load its information into a data room, it should also take care to identify who among its team will respond to specific information requests and have responsibility for management of retrieving responsive materials from the data room. In some cases, the selling company may have a comptroller, an outside accountant, and a bank with which it maintains credit facilities, each of whom may provide responses to a DD request in an uncoordinated manner. Failure to assign clear responsibility for responding to questions from buyer's team can result in an inefficient question and answer process that takes an inordinate amount of time and drives up the cost of the DD process.

*3) The Role of the Investment Banker*

The wrong investment bank and/or lack of clarity as to the banker's role in the transaction can be a serious impediment to a successful due diligence process. Problems arise when the banker prepares the initial confidential information memorandum (CIM) from materials provided by the seller, but which ultimately prove inconsistent with the materials later disclosed through the DD process. A seller is well advised to focus on whether its candidate for investment banker is ready, willing, and able to become an important and active member of the diligence team from the outset, with responsibility for making sure that the CIM it prepares for the sale process is truly consistent with the corresponding due diligence materials that will be posted to the data room.

Asking the banker to do all of that work at its own expense is unrealistic, and seller's in-house counsel or outside lawyer should also be called upon to assist. The person responsible for coordination of seller's DD process should be assigned responsibility for ensuring that the informational materials used by the banker to solicit prospective buyers, lenders, or other participants in the process are consistent with seller's due diligence materials. Failure to get this right often becomes a significant impediment to the success of the DD process. Additionally, seller's counsel should at the outset work with the banker to develop appropriate non-disclosure agreements (NDAs) for the banker to use in connection with distribution of CIMs and other materials relating to the seller or the potential transaction, taking care that the NDA contain a "non-reliance" clause designed to avoid claims of extra contractual fraud in the inducement based on information communicated to third parties by the banker, or other representatives of the seller, or which may be presented in the data room but not ultimately captured as a representation or warranty in the definitive transaction document.

*4) Confusion About Accounting Issues*

Confusion among the seller's team members over accounting issues can be extremely disruptive and a serious impediment to the DD process. Material accounting issues should be identified by the seller during its pre-process evaluation and certainly before the DD process begins. Seller's team should have a firm grasp of those issues, whether they be tax-driven by concerns of a private owner of a private company, or accounting issues driven by Generally Accepted Accounting Principles (GAAP) and audit concerns. Similarly, seller's team (or designated members of seller's team) needs to be familiar with the data underlying seller's position as to whether or not, or the extent to which, EBITDA should be adjusted one way or another, as well as any other data underlying the positions taken by seller in its financial statements, tax returns, and the CIM or other soliciting materials provided by the investment bankers.

When considering presentation of financial information, the seller needs to be mindful that it is going to be dealing with three different types of data sets, namely: financial statements, tax positions, and EBITDA summaries and calculations. These are areas where drag on the DD process can arise simply by the way in which the relevant data is presented in the data room, and the manner in which questions regarding that data are fielded by seller's team. For example, buyers can find themselves spending lots of extra time and money on outside quality of earnings consultants and other accounting firms when attempting to conduct due diligence on a private company where the seller has not differentiated among and coherently presented the three different sets of data mentioned above in a consistent narrative. This necessitates addressing, head on, any issues associated with calculation of adjusted EBITDA (e.g., add-backs) and calculations relative to tax accounting positions versus audit and GAAP accounting positions. Failure to appropriately address these three "arenas" early in the DD process often results in increased expense to both buyers and sellers, as well as delay in terms of the time required for the buyer to determine whether inconsistencies between matters revealed in data room disclosure materials on the one hand, and the financial information present in the seller's CIM or other investment banking material on the other hand, are not merely ordinary course issues, but rather are less innocent, and suggest greater risk in the transaction than the seller may have initially anticipated. Buyers are well advised to have these types of disclosures presented at the outset of DD, clearly articulated, coherently presented, and coordinated through a single "quarterback" or designated professional thoroughly familiar with the accounting issues and principles involved. At the same time, buyers faced with such a scenario should seriously consider whether proceeding further with the DD process makes sense, or whether they need to reset the process and send the seller back to the drawing board to make any appropriate adjustments needed to engage in a DD process that does not devolve into a fishing expedition to resolve competing answers or disagreements regarding calculation of EBITDA, adjusted EBITDA, tax profits, and GAAP issues.

Counsel for seller of a closely held business should early in the process seek to identify whether and how the seller's financials may be inconsistent with GAAP applied on a consistent basis, or more problematically, the extent to which the seller's accounting practices will, to support seller's valuation and purchase price, require identification of add-backs to be applied to calculation of an adjusted EBITDA. Bluntly put, before commencement of the DD process (and during the seller's internal pre-process evaluation), counsel should identify whether seller has consistently engaged in appropriate GAAP accounting, or has instead applied "family-accepted accounting principles" that need to be discussed or rectified.

Some red flags for buyers or investors when conducting DD include seller financial statements that indicate third party inter-corporate adjustments for related third party transactions; off-balance sheet transactions; and transactions with affiliated entities that are not intended to be a part of the ultimate financing or sale transaction. Uncovering this type of information should suggest to the buyer that it step back and demand that clear explanations of these items be provided by seller's CPAs before buyer deploys its own accounting professionals to research those answers. If buyer does not do so, it could end up inadvertently doing a lot of accounting work for a seller who has simply not, in its ordinary course of business, found it necessary to do so before then.

*5) Additions of Historical Documents to Data Room*

As previously suggested, another serious impediment to a successful due diligence process is having to deal with seller's ongoing supplementation of the data room, rather than ensuring that all relevant documents (or as many as reasonably possible) have been presented at the beginning of the due diligence process. Multiple professionals of different disciplines may comprise seller's diligence team and the responsibility for populating the digital data room may not have been sufficiently coordinated to ensure that all relevant information is loaded prior to the time the buyer's diligence process is set to begin. The more frequently seller adds historical documents to the data room after the process has started, the more likely that questions and concerns will be raised on the buyer's side regarding why those documents were not there to begin with.

## 6) Conflicts Between Forward Looking Statements

Problems can arise from conflicts between forward looking statements or materials reviewed in the due diligence process on the one hand, and forward looking statements found in the CIM or other materials prepared by the investment banker on the other hand (e.g., statements in relation to budgets; prior business valuations; other solicitations for information that the seller previously responded to that indicate their expectations regarding future results; prior fundraisings; and audits submitted to banks in association with loans). In many instances, the prospective buyer may have received initial forward looking information from the investment banker, such as projections prepared by the banker and the seller, which may appear to conflict with data subsequently disclosed in the DD process. Seller, before loading such materials to the data room, should determine whether or not (and why) they may appear to conflict with forward looking statements in the CIM or other materials delivered to the prospective buyer, and should provide proper qualifications and context—i.e., explaining what the data room materials and statements were actually used for by the seller at the time or times they were created and why they may appear to be inconsistent with previously delivered materials. Failure to do so can create lots of extra activity and delay the DD process.

## 7) Failure to Discuss Materiality Thresholds

Failure to discuss, and mutually agree upon, relevant materiality thresholds at the outset of the DD process can increase the time needed to complete the process and the attendant costs for both parties. Use of virtual data rooms has enabled prospective sellers to essentially effect indiscriminate "core dumps" of all of its documents, without regard to, or identification of, those that may truly be relevant to the process. An understanding between the parties as to what is and is not going to be viewed as "material" by the buyer (and to some degree capturing that in a more thoughtful DD questionnaire) can be extremely helpful in streamlining and shortening the DD process.

*8) Lack of Clear HR Records Regarding Hiring Issues*

Lack of clear, contemporaneously prepared HR records with respect to the seller's business operations and personnel can result in questions regarding compensation, benefits, hiring, retention, and other matters relevant to post closing operation of the target company. While the buyer's DD team will often inquire about the seller's HR practices and financials, they may not thoroughly explore the expectations of key personnel regarding compensation and benefits going forward, or recruiting strategies and other plans for growing the company which may ultimately prove very important to post-closing business integration.

For example, confusion (and disappointment) can arise in cases where the seller may be planning to hire additional personnel in the future, and the buyer is looking at EBITDA based on a number of personnel that have not historically been in place. When it comes out in DD that the company is planning to hire additional people, the buyer may ask whether the company was purposely understaffed by seller so as to create a higher level of EBITDA that could drive a greater valuation for the company. Seller should early on make clear what its future plans entail and why its expenses may therefore be scheduled to increase—and the best way to do that is by showing a consistent recruiting policy that existed separate and apart from the process of attempting to sell or finance the company.

*9) Lack of Coordinated Timing between Key Parties*

Lack of coordinated timing of DD queries among buyer, its consultants, and lawyers can be disruptive to the DD process. If the buyer's DD investigation is going to involve the participation and input of lender's counsel, buyer's counsel, specially retained CPAs tasked with performing a quality of earnings review, buyer's CPAs, buyer's constituents, and portfolio company CPAs, absent proper coordination, there can be a lot of duplicative inquiries, which in turn can seriously impede the DD process. Often, buyers are not as well coordinated as they should be when involving outside lenders—especially if it is a private equity buyer that also has a portfolio company with an interest in the transaction.

Lack of coordination and concomitant repetitive/duplicative requests for information can cause delays and extra expense, and create multiple opportunities for seller's personnel to be pulled off task to answer the same questions over and over again. This type of situation can get even worse if the DD process is ongoing during negotiation of transaction documents. Again, failure to properly manage the due diligence process can result in a wide range of inefficient activities, including additional and unnecessary legal and professional fees.

*10) Lack of Familiarity with Documents and Due Diligence Data*

In many cases, inefficiencies result when the investment bankers, lawyers, or even those principals of the buyer or seller tasked with negotiating the various conditions, contingencies, representations, warranties, and covenants and disclosure schedules of the transaction are unfamiliar with the parties' respective responses to the other's due diligence queries. This can result in poorly crafted transaction documents, including incomplete disclosure schedules.

The respective leaders of the buyer's and seller's teams need to make sure that the DD effort is not just a "check the box" process to be summarily ticked off to get to a closing. Rather, DD is a critical aspect of the transaction process whereby each party gains understanding of the relevant issues, tests their respective theories of the deal, identifies issues susceptible to compromise and any which are not, and ultimately determines whether or not the transaction will be consummated.

*Final Thoughts*

Each party's due diligence team should be comprised of people who have special expertise in the industry within which the seller operates. Each team should meet early on to discuss the theory of the deal, and frequently to discuss newly discovered information and whether or not that information affects the theory of the deal. They should have a clear understanding of their respective roles and responsibilities and regularly communicate with each other and the team quarterback.

Additionally, the DD process should serve to identify potential issues affecting, and a roadmap for, the post-closing integration process.

**Special Considerations and Recent Developments and Trends Affecting Due Diligence Process for Buyers**

- FCPA Compliance in Transactions Involving Sellers with Overseas Operations or Foreign Supply Chains. Over the past several years we have seen increased DD focus on compliance with the Foreign Corrupt Practices Act (FCPA).[1] Buyers considering acquisition of a business with overseas operations or supply chains will want its due diligence team to include counsel with expertise in FCPA issues, as well as a forensic accountant capable of evaluating (a) whether or not the seller actually has implemented policies for prevention and detection of foreign corrupt practices, and (b) whether those policies are being complied with.

- Human Rights. In response to public outcry following numerous human right scandals in the early 1990s, some companies (primarily in the apparel and footwear industries) developed social compliance programs to enforce minimum standards of human rights and employee health and safety in their supply chains. The outrages of the Congolese conflict resulted in passage of conflict minerals legislation.[2] The Californian Supply Chain Transparency

---

[1] 15 U.S.C. §§ 78dd-1 *et seq.* (West).
[2] *See* Dodd-Frank Wall Street Reform and Consumer Protection Act, Pub. L. No. 111-203, Sec. 1502, 124 Stat. 1376 (2010); Rule 13p-1 of the Exchange Act 17 C.F.R. 240.13p-1.

Act requires retailers or manufacturers having annual worldwide gross receipts of $100,000,000 or more to disclose their efforts to eradicate slavery and human trafficking from their direct supply chains for tangible goods offered for sale. Media attention and grassroots activism have resulted in greater awareness of human rights abuses in foreign supply chains, and in turn potential reputational damage to companies whose supply chains fail to ensure against such abuses and unfair labor practices. More recently, the collapse of the Rana Plaza garment factory in Bangladesh in 2013 and various factory fires in Pakistan again focused attention on the issue of human rights in contract manufacturing, as have controversies surrounding labor practices applied in assembly of smartphones and other devices.

- Health Care Sector Transactions. DD in transactions in the health care and medical device sectors also require evaluation of compliance with applicable state and federal law—e.g., HIPAA, Stark/anti-referral and anti-fraud and abuse laws, regulations and safe harbors.

*Anti-Trust Issues*

Counsel for competitors engaging in DD must be mindful of anti-trust concerns, and indeed anti-trust counsel should be consulted (if not also a part of the respective DD team). Care must be taken to avoid the sharing of sensitive competitive information, especially with regard to pricing. Such information should either be posted to the data room subject to restricted access protection or redacted from those materials. All such information should be reviewed by outside counsel for anti-trust compliance. The parties must keep in mind that absent proper management of this issue, potential issues or claims of collusion or gun jumping can arise, regardless of whether or not the deal closes. Special care should be taken to avoid exchange of pricing policies, marketing plans or similar specific competitively relevant information, and to avoid the sharing of such competitively relevant information with personnel responsible for formulating competitive policy.

*IP Protection*

Depending on the seller's industry, and its development or use of intellectual property assets (IP), the DD team should be comprised of IP counsel adept in the relevant technology. Special attention should be paid to gathering and review of all intellectual property assignments, employment and work for hire agreements, confidentiality agreements, and documents containing restrictive covenants between the target and third parties and all inbound and outbound licenses that the seller may be obligated under. In evaluating the seller, it is important to not only conduct interviews with management, but to also cross-check management statements against those made by personnel lower down in the organization. For example, buyer's counsel should talk to the engineers and other personnel actually engaged in the seller's IP development department to learn more about the actual development process, compliance with "clean room" protocols or other requirements imposed by relevant third-party agreements, etc.

*Environmental Issues*

In transactions where the seller's operations involve control of manufacturing, production, storage or warehouse facilities, industrial or mixed use real estate, or undeveloped land, it is important for DD to include evaluation of past and current operations at those sites, and to visit those sites to determine the existence of potential environmental issues. Phase I and possibly Phase II environmental audits may be called for.

**Representations and Warranties**

A seller should, in the definitive transaction agreement, obtain suitable representations and warranties from the buyer in situations where the transaction will involve material post-closing buyer obligations (e.g., extended payment terms, roll-over equity, earn-outs, etc.). In such situations, the seller should take care to conduct its own DD on the buyer and request appropriate representations and warranties from the buyer. If it does not do so and later finds that the buyer's post-closing performance does not meet expectations, it will likely be very hard for the seller to successfully assert claims of breach of implied representation, warranty, or common law fraud.

*Privacy Rules in Relation to the Management of Digital Assets and Cybersecurity*

The DD associated with management of digital assets in compliance with state, federal, and foreign privacy laws, and the manner in which a company manages and transfers data owned by third parties (e.g. European Union Privacy Rules, HIPAA), as well as its own sensitive data, is an issue increasingly taking center stage in recent years. We are seeing more reps and warranties addressing the absence of liabilities with respect to, and covenants associated with the management of, data, and compliance with rules regarding data privacy and data security rights of others. These days, a company may have many terabytes of stored data associated with its business, including all of the email traffic among its personnel, and there may be issues pertaining to the manner in which this data is retained. A key concern is the company's adherence to applicable regulations regarding compilation and use of such data—data that potentially belongs to employees as well as data that belongs to customers. Depending upon the level of sensitivity associated with a company's financial data, health care-related data, or other data, it is important for the buyer to tightly manage its DD questions. While the seller needs to be prepared to respond to those questions, it also needs to be aware of the applicable limits that may be imposed by law on such disclosures.

It is important for the buyer to understand the nature and scope of the target's use of software as a service (SaaS) providers for applications used in the seller's business—both from the standpoint of applications that are mission critical, as well as applications that may not seem to be that important but which may nonetheless involve capture of sensitive or regulated data. It is also important to determine whether or not such data is being properly protected, whether it is readily accessible to the seller, and the degree to which termination of a SaaS provider contract would cause a problem in terms of being able to retrieve the data in a form that could be used by the buyer to integrate and capture whatever synergies might be available from switching SaaS providers—for example, from an ERP to a CRM system. There have always been issues with respect to integrating and transitioning computer systems after acquisitions, but now that software applications are often provided by an outside service provider, neither the target nor the buyer may have control of certain data, but rather the data may be under the control of third parties. Consequently, significant costs, timing issues, and other risks attendant to these concerns need to be identified, evaluated, and managed in the DD process.

Cybersecurity has become a major global concern, as well as the focus of new government initiatives. Note, however, that the concept of information security is not new. Various laws have been on the books for years dealing with the collection, storage, and use of certain types of information. For example, the Health Insurance Portability and Accountability Act (HIPAA) addresses health-related information; the Gramm-Leach-Bliley Act addresses various aspects of financial information.[3] The Online Privacy Protection Act (COPPA) addresses collection of information from, and privacy issues attendant to, online activities of minors.[4] The FTC has enforcement authority over corporate information security practices under Section 5 of the FTC Act and various states have enacted data security regulations affecting corporate safeguards of personal information.

In February of 2013, the White House issued an Executive Order entitled "Improving Critical Infrastructure Cybersecurity" establishing requirements for owners and operators of "critical infrastructure" to develop cybersecurity frameworks, and directing that the National Institute on Standards and Technology (NIST) develop cybersecurity frameworks to reduce risks of cyber attacks to critical infrastructures. In response, the NIST in February of 2014 released its "Framework for Improving Critical Infrastructure Cybersecurity" articulating a set of industry standards and best practices to help organizations manage

---

[3] *See* Health Insurance Portability and Accountability Act, Pub. L. No. 104-191, 110 Stat. 1936 (1996); Financial Services Modernization Act of 1999, Pub. L. No. 106-102, 113 Stat 1338 (also known as the Gramm-Leach-Bliley Act).
[4] *See* 15 U.S.C. §§ 6501-06 (West).

cybersecurity risks. The Executive Order defines critical infrastructure as "systems and assets, physical or virtual, so vital to the United States that the incapacity or destruction of such systems and assets would have a debilitating impact on security, national economic security, national public health or safety, or any combination of those matters." While the "Framework" was initially intended as a voluntary program, one may expect to see federal contracting incentives used to encourage private sector compliance, and possibly the evolution of a basic "community standard" from, or incorporating, the Framework. Additionally, in April of 2014, the Office of Compliance Inspections and Examinations (OCIE) of the SEC announced, via a Risk Alert, that it will be conducting cybersecurity examinations of fifty registered investment advisors and broker dealers as part of an initiative to assess cybersecurity preparedness in the securities industry. The OCIE has promulgated a sample document request in its Risk Alert which sets forth areas subject to the OCIE's evaluation—namely, cybersecurity governance and identification and assessment of cybersecurity risks; protection of networks and information; risks associated with remote customer access and funds transfer requests; risks associated with vendors/third parties; detection of unauthorized activity; and experience with various specified cybersecurity threats. This movement by federal agencies toward establishment of best practice standards in cybersecurity preparedness will likely increase, and may be expected to result in the buyer's DD process incorporating some evaluation of whether seller's network security practices comply with applicable standards/best practices.

## Conclusion

An effective and successful due diligence process ultimately requires that the parties and their respective counsel thoughtfully prepare for the process, consider the reasons for the contemplated transaction, any key issues that might materially impair the value of the transaction, and deploy the appropriate personnel to seek out and evaluate truly relevant information. Identifying early in the process the key players who will comprise the due diligence team is crucial. That team should develop protocols for interacting among themselves as well as with their opposite numbers, so as to streamline the DD process and avoid unnecessary delay, confusion, and attendant run-up in costs. The industry in which the target operates, and the regulatory environment, will also dictate the contours of due diligence inquiries. At the end of the day, however, there is no substitute for strong preparation, common sense, good will, and knowledge of the relevant subject matter, including the legal, accounting, regulatory, and market issues.

**Key Takeaways**

- A seller that understands what to expect from the due diligence process and has a good grasp of where its records are and what type of accounting it has engaged in, and has kept track of and indexed its important records and agreements, is more likely to successfully negotiate its way through the due diligence process.

- Assist the seller in assembling a due diligence team and a digital data room. Make sure that the internal team leader obtains all necessary information in a timely and efficient manner; inputs it into the protected digital environment; and properly indexes it, and segregates it to the extent that there may be more than one level of confidentiality. Do not underestimate the importance of a proper diligence team, obtaining the right information, and creating a clear plan with respect to who will respond to the buyer's questions and provide real-time management of key issues. Typically, the seller's investment banker and lawyer should play a central role in managing this process, along with one key leader from the company, so that inefficiencies are avoided and the seller has a realistic view of the resources required.

- Ensure that the seller's banker becomes an important part of the diligence team from the beginning, and is responsible for making sure that the confidential information memorandum they prepare in connection with the transaction is consistent with the seller's actual records and thus the due diligence that is ultimately obtained.

- Discuss materiality thresholds in relation to due diligence. Absent mutual agreement as to materiality, the advent of widespread use of virtual data rooms often results in the seller doing a "core dump" of all of its documents. This in turn can lead to a longer, inefficient, and more costly DD process. Keep in mind that the DD team needs to be comprised of people who have expertise in the industry within which the seller operates; they should meet early on and frequently to discuss matters discovered in DD and the evolving theory of the transaction. They should have a clear understanding of their respective roles and regularly communicate with the team quarterback. Finally, they should identify how the post-closing integration process will take place.

- In transactions involving foreign operations or supply chains, work with specialists, including a forensic accountant who can identify FCPA issues. In transactions involving sellers engaged in development of IP assets, IP counsel should evaluate whether the seller has all the IP rights it says it does.

*Michael G. Platner a partner with Lewis Brisbois Bisgaard & Smith LLP, serves as chair of the firm's Corporate Practice Group. Mr. Platner enjoys solving problems and developing business savvy legal strategies for business clients, their owners and investors. Mr. Platner also has founded or been an early stage investor in several businesses, particularly in software, Internet infrastructure, and cloud computing. Empathizing with the role of the client, he believes that a transactional lawyer adds the most value by fully understanding the business strategy and the "deal" so as to be able to suggest creative strategies and alternatives. Mr. Platner also manages litigation matters strategically in the context of how the ultimate business goals can best be achieved and financial statement impacts considered. His practice is focused on helping companies and their owners build value and manage risk.*

*Solomon B. Zoberman is a partner in Lewis Brisbois Bisgaard & Smith LLP's Fort Lauderdale office who focuses his practice on business law, litigation, and intellectual property. Before joining Lewis Brisbois, Mr. Zoberman had been in private practice since 1982. He has experience in advising closely held corporations, limited liability companies and other business entities on issues of governance, shareholder or member relations, executive compensation, employment issues, restrictive covenants and secured transactions; intellectual property with emphasis on trademark, copyright, trade secrets, and computer software development, licensing and distribution; real estate, with emphasis on commercial leasing; and mergers and acquisitions.*

# APPENDICES

Appendix A: Example of Selected Seller
Representations and Warranties                    80

Appendix B: 15 U.S.C.A. § 78dd-1                  82

## APPENDIX A

## EXAMPLE OF SELECTED SELLER REPRESENTATIONS AND WARRANTIES

Except as set forth in Section __, since the date of the balance sheet, Seller has conducted its business only in the ordinary course of business and there has not been any (a) entry into, termination of, or receipt of notice of termination of any contract or transaction involving a total remaining commitment by Seller of at least $_____; or (b) indication by any customer or supplier of an intention to discontinue or change the terms of its relationship with Seller.

No contract which is to be assigned to or assumed by Buyer under this Agreement will, upon completion or performance thereof, have a material adverse effect on the business, assets or condition of Seller or the business to be conducted by Buyer with the assets.

No event has occurred or circumstance exists that (with or without notice or lapse of time) may contravene, conflict with or result in a breach of, or give Seller or other person the right to declare a default or exercise any remedy under, or to accelerate the maturity or performance of, or payment under, or to cancel, terminate or modify, any Seller contract that is being assigned to or assumed by Buyer.

There are no renegotiations of, attempts to renegotiate or outstanding rights to renegotiate any material amounts paid or payable to Seller under current or completed contracts with any person having the contractual or statutory right to demand or require such renegotiation, and no such person has made written demand for such renegotiation.

No representation or warranty or other statement made by Seller in this Agreement contains any material untrue statement or omits to state a material fact necessary to make any of them, in light of the circumstances in which it was made, not misleading.

Seller does not have knowledge of any fact that has specific application to the Seller (other than general economic or industry conditions) and that may materially adversely affect the assets, business, prospects, financial condition, or results of operations of Seller that has not been set forth in this agreement.

*Courtesy of James A. Butz, Frost Brown Todd LLC*

# APPENDIX B

## 15 U.S.C.A. § 78DD-1

**Effective: November 10, 1998**

United States Code Annotated Currentness

Title 15. Commerce and Trade

Chapter 2B. Securities Exchanges (Refs & Annos)

### § 78dd-1. Prohibited foreign trade practices by issuers

(a)  Prohibition

It shall be unlawful for any issuer which has a class of securities registered pursuant to section 78*l* of this title or which is required to file reports under section 78*o*(d) of this title, or for any officer, director, employee, or agent of such issuer or any stockholder thereof acting on behalf of such issuer, to make use of the mails or any means or instrumentality of interstate commerce corruptly in furtherance of an offer, payment, promise to pay, or authorization of the payment of any money, or offer, gift, promise to give, or authorization of the giving of anything of value to--

(1)  any foreign official for purposes of--

    A.  (i) influencing any act or decision of such foreign official in his official capacity, (ii) inducing such foreign official to do or omit to do any act in violation of the lawful duty of such official, or (iii) securing any improper advantage; or
    B.  inducing such foreign official to use his influence with a foreign government or instrumentality thereof to affect or influence any act or decision of such government or instrumentality,

in order to assist such issuer in obtaining or retaining business for or with, or directing business to, any person;

(2) any foreign political party or official thereof or any candidate for foreign political office for purposes of--

A. (i) influencing any act or decision of such party, official, or candidate in its or his official capacity, (ii) inducing such party, official, or candidate to do or omit to do an act in violation of the lawful duty of such party, official, or candidate, or (iii) securing any improper advantage; or

B. inducing such party, official, or candidate to use its or his influence with a foreign government or instrumentality thereof to affect or influence any act or decision of such government or instrumentality.

in order to assist such issuer in obtaining or retaining business for or with, or directing business to, any person; or

(3) any person, while knowing that all or a portion of such money or thing of value will be offered, given, or promised, directly or indirectly, to any foreign official, to any foreign political party or official thereof, or to any candidate for foreign political office, for purposes of--

A. (i) influencing any act or decision of such foreign official, political party, party official, or candidate in his or its official capacity, (ii) inducing such foreign official, political party, party official, or candidate to do or omit to do any act in violation of the lawful duty of such foreign official, political party, party official, or candidate, or (iii) securing any improper advantage; or

B. inducing such foreign official, political party, party official, or candidate to use his or its influence with a foreign government or instrumentality thereof to affect or influence any act or decision of such government or instrumentality,

in order to assist such issuer in obtaining or retaining business for or with, or directing business to, any person.

(b)  Exception for routine governmental action

Subsections (a) and (g) of this section shall not apply to any facilitating or expediting payment to a foreign official, political party, or party official the purpose of which is to expedite or to secure the performance of a routine governmental action by a foreign official, political party, or party official.

(c)  Affirmative defenses

It shall be an affirmative defense to actions under subsection (a) or (g) of this section that--

(1)  the payment, gift, offer, or promise of anything of value that was made, was lawful under the written laws and regulations of the foreign official's, political party's, party official's, or candidate's country; or

(2)  the payment, gift, offer, or promise of anything of value that was made, was a reasonable and bona fide expenditure, such as travel and lodging expenses, incurred by or on behalf of a foreign official, party, party official, or candidate and was directly related to--

(A)  the promotion, demonstration, or explanation of products or services; or

(B)  the execution or performance of a contract with a foreign government or agency thereof.

(d)  Guidelines by Attorney General

Not later than one year after August 23, 1988, the Attorney General, after consultation with the Commission, the Secretary of Commerce, the United States Trade Representative, the Secretary of State, and the Secretary of the Treasury, and after obtaining the views of all interested persons through public notice and comment procedures, shall determine to what extent compliance with this section would be enhanced and the business community would be assisted by further clarification of the preceding provisions of this section and may, based on such determination and to the extent necessary and appropriate, issue--

(1) guidelines describing specific types of conduct, associated with common types of export sales arrangements and business contracts, which for purposes of the Department of Justice's present enforcement policy, the Attorney General determines would be in conformance with the preceding provisions of this section; and

(2) general precautionary procedures which issuers may use on a voluntary basis to conform their conduct to the Department of Justice's present enforcement policy regarding the preceding provisions of this section.

The Attorney General shall issue the guidelines and procedures referred to in the preceding sentence in accordance with the provisions of subchapter II of chapter 5 of Title 5 and those guidelines and procedures shall be subject to the provisions of chapter 7 of that title.

(e) Opinions of Attorney General

(1) The Attorney General, after consultation with appropriate departments and agencies of the United States and after obtaining the views of all interested persons through public notice and comment procedures, shall establish a procedure to provide responses to specific inquiries by issuers concerning conformance of their conduct with the Department of Justice's present enforcement policy regarding the preceding provisions of this section. The Attorney General shall, within 30 days after receiving such a request, issue an opinion in response to that request. The opinion shall state whether or not certain specified prospective conduct would, for purposes of the Department of Justice's present enforcement policy, violate the preceding provisions of this section. Additional requests for opinions may be filed with the Attorney General regarding other specified prospective conduct that is beyond the scope of conduct specified in previous requests. In any action brought under the applicable provisions of this section, there shall be a rebuttable presumption that conduct, which is specified in a request by an issuer and for which the Attorney General has issued an opinion that such conduct is in conformity with the Department of

Justice's present enforcement policy, is in compliance with the preceding provisions of this section. Such a presumption may be rebutted by a preponderance of the evidence. In considering the presumption for purposes of this paragraph, a court shall weight all relevant factors, including but not limited to whether the information submitted to the Attorney General was accurate and complete and whether it was within the scope of the conduct specified in any request received by the Attorney General. The Attorney General shall establish the procedure required by this paragraph in accordance with the provisions of subchapter II of chapter 5 of Title 5 and that procedure shall be subject to the provisions of chapter 7 of that title.

(2) Any document or other material which is provided to, received by, or prepared in the Department of Justice or any other department or agency of the United States in connection with a request by an issuer under the procedure established under paragraph (1), shall be exempt from disclosure under section 552 of Title 5 and shall not, except with the consent of the issuer, be made publicly available, regardless of whether the Attorney General responds to such a request or the issuer withdraws such request before receiving a response.

(3) Any issuer who has made a request to the Attorney General under paragraph (1) may withdraw such request prior to the time the Attorney General issues an opinion in response to such request. Any request so withdrawn shall have no force or effect.

(4) The Attorney General shall, to the maximum extent practicable, provide timely guidance concerning the Department of Justice's present enforcement policy with respect to the preceding provisions of this section to potential exporters and small businesses that are unable to obtain specialized counsel on issues pertaining to such provisions. Such guidance shall be limited to responses to requests under paragraph (1) concerning conformity of specified prospective conduct with the Department of Justice's present enforcement policy regarding the preceding provisions of this section and general explanations of compliance responsibilities and of potential liabilities under the preceding provisions of this section.

(f) Definitions

For purposes of this section:

1.

    A. The term "foreign official" means any officer or employee of a foreign government or any department, agency, or instrumentality thereof, or of a public international organization, or any person acting in an official capacity for or on behalf of any such government or department, agency, or instrumentality, or for or on behalf of any such public international organization.

    B. For purposes of subparagraph (A), the term "public international organization" means--

        1. an organization that is designated by Executive order pursuant to section 1 of the International Organizations Immunities Act (22 U.S.C. 288); or

        2. any other international organization that is designated by the President by Executive order for the purposes of this section, effective as of the date of publication of such order in the Federal Register.

2.

    1. A person's state of mind is "knowing" with respect to conduct, a circumstance, or a result if--

        (i) such person is aware that such person is engaging in such conduct, that such circumstance exists, or that such result is substantially certain to occur; or

        (ii) such person has a firm belief that such circumstance exists or that such result is substantially certain to occur.

    2. When knowledge of the existence of a particular circumstance is required for an offense, such knowledge is established if a person is aware of a high probability of the existence of such

circumstance, unless the person actually believes that such circumstance does not exist.

3.

A. The term "routine governmental action" means only an action which is ordinarily and commonly performed by a foreign official in--

   (i) obtaining permits, licenses, or other official documents to qualify a person to do business in a foreign country;
   (ii) processing governmental papers, such as visas and work orders;
   (iii) providing police protection, mail pick-up and delivery, or scheduling inspections associated with contract performance or inspections related to transit of goods across country;
   (iv) providing phone service, power and water supply, loading and unloading cargo, or protecting perishable products or commodities from deterioration; or
   (v) actions of a similar nature.

B. The term "routine governmental action" does not include any decision by a foreign official whether, or on what terms, to award new business to or to continue business with a particular party, or any action taken by a foreign official involved in the decision-making process to encourage a decision to award new business to or continue business with a particular party.

(g) Alternative jurisdiction

   (1) It shall also be unlawful for any issuer organized under the laws of the United States, or a State, territory, possession, or commonwealth of the United States or a political subdivision thereof and which has a class of securities registered pursuant to section 78*l* of this title or which is required to file reports under section 78*o*(d) of this title, or for any United States person that is an officer, director, employee, or agent of such issuer or a

stockholder thereof acting on behalf of such issuer, to corruptly do any act outside the United States in furtherance of an offer, payment, promise to pay, or authorization of the payment of any money, or offer, gift, promise to give, or authorization of the giving of anything of value to any of the persons or entities set forth in paragraphs (1), (2), and (3) of subsection (a) of this section for the purposes set forth therein, irrespective of whether such issuer or such officer, director, employee, agent, or stockholder makes use of the mails or any means or instrumentality of interstate commerce in furtherance of such offer, gift, payment, promise, or authorization.

(2) As used in this subsection, the term "United States person" means a national of the United States (as defined in section 101 of the Immigration and Nationality Act (8 U.S.C. 1101)) or any corporation, partnership, association, joint-stock company, business trust, unincorporated organization, or sole proprietorship organized under the laws of the United States or any State, territory, possession, or commonwealth of the United States, or any political subdivision thereof.

CREDIT(S)

(June 6, 1934, c. 404, Title I, § 30A, as added Dec. 19, 1977, Pub.L. 95-213, Title I, § 103(a), 91 Stat. 1495; amended Aug. 23, 1988, Pub.L. 100-418, Title V, § 5003(a), 102 Stat. 1415; Nov. 10, 1998, Pub.L. 105-366, § 2(a) to (c), 112 Stat. 3302.)

HISTORICAL AND STATUTORY NOTES

Revision Notes and Legislative Reports

- 1977 Acts. Senate Report No. 95-114 and House Conference Report No. 95-831, see 1977 U.S. Code Cong. and Adm. News, p. 4098.
- 1988 Acts. House Conference Report No. 100-576, see 1988 U.S. Code Cong. and Adm. News, p. 1547.

Amendments

- 1998 Amendments. Subsec. (a)(1)(A). Pub.L. 105-366, § 2(a)(1), rewrote subpar. (A) which formerly read: **"(A)**(i) influencing any act or decision of such foreign official in his official capacity, or (ii) inducing such foreign official to do or omit to do any act in violation of the lawful duty of such official, or"

- Subsec. (a)(2)(A). Pub.L. 105-366, § 2(a)(2), rewrote subpar. (A) which formerly read: **"(A)**(i) influencing any act or decision of such party, official, or candidate in its or his official capacity, or (ii) inducing such party, official, or candidate to do or omit to do an act in violation of the lawful duty of such party, official, or candidate,"

- Subsec. (a)(3)(A). Pub.L. 105-366, § 2(a)(3), rewrote subpar. (A) which formerly read: **"(A)**(i) influencing any act or decision of such foreign official, political party, party official, or candidate in his or its official capacity, or (ii) inducing such foreign official, political party, party official, or candidate to do or omit to do any act in violation of the lawful duty of such foreign official, political party, party official, or candidate, or"

- Subsec. (b). Pub.L. 105-366, § 2(c)(2), struck "Subsection (a)" and inserted "Subsections (a) and (g)".

- Subsec. (c). Pub.L. 105-366, § 2(c)(3), struck "subsection (a)" and inserted "subsection (a) or (g)".

- Subsec. (f)(1). Pub.L. 105-366, § 2(b), rewrote par. (1) which formerly read: **"(1)** The term 'foreign official' means any officer or employee of a foreign government or any department, agency, or instrumentality thereof, or any person acting in an official capacity for or on behalf of any such government or department, agency, or instrumentality."

- Subsec. (g). Pub.L. 105-366, § 2(c)(1), added subsec. (g).

- 1988 Amendments. Catchline. Pub.L. 100-418, § 5003(a), substituted "Prohibited foreign trade practices by issuers" for "Foreign corrupt practices by issuers".

- Subsec. (a). Catchline. Pub.L. 100-418, § 5003(a), substituted "Prohibition" for "Prohibited practices".

- Subsec. (a)(1)(A). Pub.L. 100-418, § 5003(a), divided subpar. (A) into cls. (i) and (ii), and in cl. (ii), as so designated substituted "inducing such foreign official to do or omit to do any act in violation of the lawful duty of such official, or" for "including a decision to fail to perform his official functions; or".

- Subsec. (a)(2)(A). Pub.L. 100-418, § 5003(a), divided subpar. (A) into cls. (i) and (ii), and in cl. (ii), as so designated substituted "inducing such party, official, or candidate to do or omit to do an act in violation of the lawful duty of such party, official, or candidate," for "including a decision to fail to perform its or his official functions; or".

- Subsec. (a)(3). Pub.L. 100-418, § 5003(c), in provisions preceding subpar. (A) substituted "while knowing that all" for "while knowing or having reason to know that all", and in subpar. (A) divided existing provisions into cls. (i) and (ii), and in cl. (ii), as so designated, substituted "inducing such foreign official, political party, party official, or candidate to do or omit to do any act in violation of the lawful duty of such foreign official, political party, party official, or candidate, or" for "including a decision to fail to perform his or its official functions; or".

- Subsec. (b). Pub.L. 100-418, § 5003(a), added subsec. (b). Former subsec. (b) redesignated (f).

- Subsec. (c). Pub.L. 100-418, § 5003(a), added subsec. (c).

- Subsec. (d). Pub.L. 100-418, § 5003(a), added subsec. (d).

- Subsec. (e). Pub.L. 100-418, § 5003(a), added subsec. (e).

- Subsec. (f). Pub.L. 100-418, § 5003(a), redesignated former subsec. (b) as (f), in subsec. (f), as so redesignated, designated existing provisions in part as par. (1), in par. (1) as so designated struck out provision that the term "foreign official" did not include any employee of a foreign government or any department, agency, or instrumentality thereof whose duties were essentially ministerial or clerical, and added pars. (2) and (3).

Treatment of International Organizations Providing Commercial Communications Services

Pub.L. 105-366, § 5, Nov. 10, 1998, 112 Stat. 3309, provided that:

(a) **Definition.**--For purposes of this section:

  (1) **International organization providing commercial communications services.**--The term 'international organization providing commercial communications services' means--

    A. the International Telecommunications Satellite Organization established pursuant to the Agreement Relating to the International Telecommunications Satellite Organization; and
    B. the International Mobile Satellite Organization established pursuant to the Convention on the International Maritime Satellite Organization.

  (2) **Pro-competitive privatization.**--The term 'pro-competitive privatization' means a privatization that the President determines to be consistent with the United States policy of obtaining full and open competition to such organizations (or their successors), and nondiscriminatory market access, in the provision of satellite services.

(b) **Treatment as public international organizations.**--

  (1) **Treatment.**--An international organization providing commercial communications services shall be treated as a public international organization for purposes of section 30A of the Securities Exchange Act of 1934 (15 U.S.C. 78dd-1) and sections 104 and 104A of the Foreign Corrupt Practices Act of 1977 (15 U.S.C. 78dd-2 [and 78dd-3]) until such time as the President certifies to the Committee on Commerce of the House of Representatives and the Committees on Banking, Housing and Urban Affairs and Commerce, Science, and Transportation that such international organization providing commercial communications services has achieved a pro-competitive privatization.

  (2) **Limitation on effect of treatment.**--The requirement for a certification under paragraph (1), and any certification made under such paragraph, shall not be construed to affect the administration by the Federal Communications Commission of the Communications Act of 1934 [June 19, 1934, c. 652, 48 Stat. 1064, classified principally at 47 U.S.C.A. § 151 et seq., for

complete classification, see Tables] in authorizing the provision of services to, from, or within the United States over space segment of the international satellite organizations, or the privatized affiliates or successors thereof.

(c) **Extension of legal process.**--

(1) **In general.**--Except as required by international agreements to which the United States is a party, an international organization providing commercial communications services, its officials and employees, and its records shall not be accorded immunity from suit or legal process for any act or omission taken in connection with such organization's capacity as a provider, directly or indirectly, of commercial telecommunications services to, from, or within the United States.

(2) **No effect on personal liability.**--Paragraph (1) shall not affect any immunity from personal liability of any individual who is an official or employee of an international organization providing commercial communications services.

(3) **Effective date.**--This subsection shall take effect on May 1, 1999.

(d) **Elimination or limitation of exceptions.**--

(1) **Action required.**--The President shall, in a manner that is consistent with requirements in international agreements to which the United States is a party, expeditiously take all appropriate actions necessary to eliminate or to reduce substantially all privileges and immunities that are accorded to an international organization described in subparagraph (A) or (B) of subsection (a)(1), its officials, its employees, or its records, and that are not eliminated pursuant to subsection (c).

(2) **Designation of agreements.**--The President shall designate which agreements constitute international agreements to which the United States is a party for purposes of this section.

(e) **Preservation of law enforcement and intelligence functions.**--Nothing in subsection (c) or (d) of this section shall affect any immunity from suit or legal process of an international organization providing commercial communications services, or the privatized affiliates or successors thereof, for acts or omissions—

(1) under chapter 119 [18 U.S.C.A. § 2510 et seq.], 121 [18 U.S.C.A. § 2701 et seq.], 206 [18 U.S.C.A. § 3121 et seq.], or 601 [18 U.S.C.A. § 6001 et seq.] of title 18, United States Code, the Foreign Intelligence Surveillance Act of 1978 (50 U.S.C. 1801 et seq.), section 514 of the Comprehensive Drug Abuse Prevention and Control Act of 1970 (21 U.S.C. 884), or Rule 104, 501, or 608 of the Federal Rules of Evidence;

(2) under similar State laws providing protection to service providers cooperating with law enforcement agencies pursuant to State electronic surveillance or evidence laws, rules, regulations, or procedures; or

(3) pursuant to a court order.

(f) **Rules of construction.--**

(1) **Negotiations.--**Nothing in this section shall affect the President's existing constitutional authority regarding the time, scope, and objectives of international negotiations.

(2) **Privatization.--**Nothing in this section shall be construed as legislative authorization for the privatization of INTELSAT or INMARSAT, nor to increase the President's authority with respect to negotiations concerning such privatization."

[For delegation of authority under section 5(d)(2) of Pub.L. 105-366 [subsec. (d)(2) of this note], see Memorandum of the President, Nov. 16, 1998, 63 F.R. 65597, set out as a note under this section.]

Enforcement and Monitoring

Pub.L. 105-366, § 6, Nov. 10, 1998, 112 Stat. 3311, provided that:

(a) **Reports required.--**Not later than July 1 of 1999 and each of the 5 succeeding years, the Secretary of Commerce shall submit to the House of Representatives and the Senate a report that contains the following information with respect to implementation of the Convention:

(1) **Ratification.**--A list of the countries that have ratified the Convention, the dates of ratification by such countries, and the entry into force for each such country.

(2) **Domestic legislation.**--A description of domestic laws enacted by each party to the Convention that implement commitments under the Convention, and assessment of the compatibility of such laws with the Convention.

(3) **Enforcement.**--As assessment of the measures taken by each party to the Convention during the previous year to fulfill its obligations under the Convention and achieve its object and purpose including--

   A. an assessment of the enforcement of the domestic laws described in paragraph (2);

   B. an assessment of the efforts by each such party to promote public awareness of such domestic laws and the achievement of such object and purpose; and

   C. an assessment of the effectiveness, transparency, and viability of the monitoring process for the Convention, including its inclusion of input from the private sector and nongovernmental organizations.

(4) **Laws prohibiting tax deduction of bribes.**--An explanation of the domestic laws enacted by each party to the Convention that would prohibit the deduction of bribes in the computation of domestic taxes.

(5) **New signatories.**--A description of efforts to expand international participation in the Convention by adding new signatories to the Convention and by assuring that all countries which are or become members of the Organization for Economic Cooperation and Development are also parties to the Convention.

(6) **Subsequent efforts**--An assessment of the status of efforts to strengthen the Convention by extending the prohibitions contained in the Convention to cover bribes to political parties, party officials, and candidates for political office.

(7) **Advantages.**--Advantages, in terms of immunities, market access, or otherwise, in the countries or regions served by the organizations described in section 5(a) [of Pub.L. 105-366, classified to 15 U.S.C.A. 78dd-1 note], the reason for such advantages, and an assessment of progress toward fulfilling the policy described in that section.

(8) **Bribery and transparency.**--An assessment of anti-bribery programs and

transparency with respect to each of the international organizations covered by this Act [International Anti-Bribery and Fair Competition Act of 1998, Pub.L. 105-366, Nov. 10, 1998, 112 Stat. 3302].

(9) **Private sector review.**--A description of the steps taken to ensure full involvement of United States private sector participants and representatives of nongovernmental organizations in the monitoring and implementation of the Convention.

(10) **Additional information.**--In consultation with the private sector participants and representatives of nongovernmental organizations described in paragraph (9), a list of additional means for enlarging the scope of the Convention and otherwise increasing its effectiveness. Such additional means shall include, but not be limited to, improved recordkeeping provisions and the desirability of expanding the applicability of the Convention to additional individuals and organizations and the impact on United States business of section 30A of the Securities Exchange Act of 1934 [section 78dd-1 of this title] and sections 104 and 104A of the Foreign Corrupt Practices Act of 1977 [sections 78dd-2 and 78dd-3 of this title].

(b) **Definition.**--For purposes of this section, the term 'Convention' means the Convention on Combating Bribery of Foreign Public Officials in International Business Transactions adopted on November 21, 1997, and signed on December 17, 1997, by the United States and 32 other nations."

Internal Agreements Concerning Acts Prohibited With Respect to Issuers and Domestic Concerns; Report to Congress

Section 5003(d) of Pub.L. 100-418 provided that:

(1) **Negotiations.**--It is the sense of the Congress that the President should pursue the negotiation of an international agreement, among the members of the Organization of Economic Cooperation and Development, to govern persons from those countries concerning acts prohibited with respect to issuers and domestic concerns by the amendments made by this section [amending sections 78dd-1, 78dd-2, and 78ff of this title]. Such

international agreement should include a process by which problems and conflicts associated with such acts could be resolved.

(2) **Report to Congress.—**

A. Within 1 year after the date of the enactment of this Act [Aug. 23, 1988], the President shall submit to the Congress a report on--

    (i) the progress of the negotiations referred to in paragraph (1),

    (ii) those steps which the executive branch and the Congress should consider taking in the event that these negotiations do not successfully eliminate any competitive disadvantage of United States businesses that results when persons from other countries commit the acts described in paragraph (1); and

    (iii) possible actions that could be taken to promote cooperation by other countries in international efforts to prevent bribery of foreign officials, candidates, or parties in third countries.

B. The President shall include in the report submitted under subparagraph (A)--

    (i) any legislative recommendations necessary to give the President the authority to take appropriate action to carry out clauses (ii) and (iii) of subparagraph (A);

    (ii) an analysis of the potential effect on the interests of the United States, including United States national security, when persons from other countries commit the acts described in paragraph (1); and

    (iii) an assessment of the current and future role of private initiatives in curtailing such acts."

EXECUTIVE ORDERS

EXECUTIVE ORDER NO. 13259

<March 19, 2002, 67 F.R. 13239>

ORGANIZATIONS FOR PURPOSES OF THE SECURITIES EXCHANGE ACT OF 1934 AND THE FOREIGN CORRUPT PRACTICES ACT OF 1977

By the authority vested in me as President by the Constitution and the laws of the United States of America, including section 30A(f)(1)(B)(ii) of the Securities Exchange Act of 1934 (15 U.S.C. 78dd-1(f)(1)(B)(ii)) and sections 104(h)(2)(B)(ii) and 104A(f)(2)(B)(ii) of the Foreign Corrupt Practices Act of 1977 (15 U.S.C. 78dd-2(h)(2)(B)(ii), 78dd-3(f)(2)(B) (ii)), I hereby designate as "public international organizations" for the purposes of application of section 30A of the Securities Exchange Act of 1934 and sections 104 and 104A of the Foreign Corrupt Practices Act of 1977:

(a) The European Union, including: the European Communities (the European Community, the European Coal & Steel Community, and the European Atomic Energy Community); institutions of the European Union, such as the European Commission, the Council of the European Union, the European Parliament, the European Court of Justice, the European Court of Auditors, the Economic and Social Committee, the Committee of the Regions, the European Central Bank, and the European Investment Bank; and any departments, agencies, and instrumentalities thereof; and

(b) The European Police Office (Europol), including any departments, agencies, and instrumentalities thereof.

Designation in this Executive Order is intended solely to further the purposes of the statutes mentioned above and is not determinative of whether an entity is a public international organization for the purpose of other statutes or regulations.

GEORGE W. BUSH

MEMORANDA OF PRESIDENT

Delegation of Authority Under Section 5(d)(2) of the International Anti-Bribery and Fair Competition Act of 1998

Memoranda of President, Nov. 16, 1998, 63 F.R. 65997, delegated to the Secretary of State the functions and authorities vested in the President by section 5(d)(2) of the International Anti-Bribery and Fair Competition Act of 1998 (Public Law 105-366).

CROSS REFERENCES

- Arms export licensing, identification of persons convicted or subject to indictment for violations under this section, see 22 USCA § 2778.
- Income tax deduction not allowed for unlawful payment under this section, see 26 USCA § 162.
- Income tax provisions relating to controlled foreign corporations,

  o Payments unlawful under this section if payor were United States person not taken into account to decrease earnings and profits or to increase deficit, see 26 USCA § 964.
  o "Subpart F income" defined as including payments unlawful under this section if payor were United States person, see 26 USCA § 952.

- Overseas Private Investment Corporation, prohibition on insurance or reinsurance payments for losses resulting from act constituting violation of this section, see 22 USCA § 2197.
- Refusal, suspension or revocation of registration of commodity dealers and associated persons found in proceeding to have violated this section, see 7 USCA § 12a.
- "Specified unlawful activity" defined as any felony violation under this section for purposes of crime of laundering of monetary instruments, see 18 USCA § 1956.

FEDERAL SENTENCING GUIDELINES

- See Federal Sentencing Guidelines § 2B4.1, 18 USCA.

LAW REVIEW COMMENTARIES

- Ambiguities in the Foreign Corrupt Practices ACT: Unnecessary costs of fighting corruption? Comment, 61 La.L.Rev. 861 Louisiana Law Review (2001).

- Avoiding criminal liability in the conduct of international business. Bruce Zagaris, 21 Wm.Mitchell L.Rev. 749 (1996).
- Bibliography on the Foreign Corrupt Practices Act of 1977. Steven C. Perkins, 14 W.St.U.L.Rev. 491 (1987).
- Bribery in economies in transition: Foreign Corrupt Practices Act. Agnieszka Klich, 32 Stan.J.Int'l L. 121 (1996).
- Exposure to the Foreign Corrupt Practices Act: A guide for U.S. companies with activities in the People's Republic of China to minimize liability. 19 Hastings Int'l & Comp.L.Rev. 327 (1996).
- The Foreign Corrupt Practices Act and clinical trials: A trap for the unwary. Drew A. Harker and Chad E. Miller, 63 Food & Drug L.J. 509 (2008).
- Foreign Corrupt Practices Act. Pamela J. Jadwin and Monica Shilling, 31 Am.Crim.L.Rev. 677 (1994).
- Foreign Corrupt Practices Act. 7 S.C.Law. 39 (March-April 1996).
- Foreign Corrupt Practices Act Amendments: The Omnibus Trade and Competitiveness Act's focus on improving investment opportunities. Beverley H. Earle, 37 Clev.St.L.Rev. 549 (1989).
- The Foreign Corrupt Practices Act, international norms of foreign public bribery, and extraterritorial jurisdiction. Evan P. Lestelle, 83 Tul.L.Rev. 527 (2008).
- New initiatives for foreign issuers. Roberta S. Karmel, 210 N.Y.L.J. 3 (Dec. 16, 1993).
- Newly amended Foreign Corrupt Practices Act. Stephen J. DeCosse and Susan S. Katcher, 63 Wis.Law. 23 (July 1990).
- Placing the Foreign Corrupt Practices Act on the tracks in the race for amnesty. 90 Tex. L. Rev. 1009 (2012).
- Prescriptions for compliance with the Foreign Corrupt Practices Act: Identifying bribery risks and implementing anti-bribery controls in pharmaceutical and life sciences companies. Roger M. Witten, Kimberly A. Parker, Jay Holtmeier, Thomas J. Koffer, 64 Bus. Law. 691 (2009).
- Private FCPA enforcement. Gideon Mark, 49 Am. Bus. L.J. 419 (2012).
- Sheep in wolf's clothing: The American law institute principles of corporate governance project. Joel Seligman, 55 Geo.Wash.L.Rev. 325 (1987).

- Toward a Reg. FCPA: A Modest Proposal for Change in Administering the Foreign Corrupt Practices Act. James R. Doty, 62 Bus. Law. 1233 (2007).
- Under the FCPA, who is a foreign official anyway? Joel M. Cohen, Michael P. Holland and Adam P. Wolf, 63 Bus. Law. 1243 (August 2008).

## LIBRARY REFERENCES

American Digest System

- Securities Regulation 30.10 to 30.15, 67.10 to 67.15.
- Key Number System Topic No. 349B.

Corpus Juris Secundum

- CJS Corporations § 500, Pleading.
- CJS Corporations § 500, Pleading.
- CJS Criminal Law § 2336, Requisites and Sufficiency of Judgment or Sentence.
- CJS Criminal Law § 2336, Requisites and Sufficiency of Judgment or Sentence.
- CJS International Law § 34, International Comity; Statutory Provisions.
- CJS International Law § 34, International Comity; Statutory Provisions.

## RESEARCH REFERENCES

ALR Library

- 6 ALR, Fed. 2nd Series 351, Construction and Application of Foreign Corrupt Practices Act of 1977.
- 44 ALR, Fed. 627, Admissibility of Statement by Coconspirator Under Rule 801(D)(2)(E) of Federal Rules of Evidence.
- 121 ALR, Fed. 323, Increase in Base Offense Level Under Sentencing Guidelines § 3B1.3 (U.S.S.G. § 3B1.3) for Abuse of Position of Public or Private Trust Significantly Facilitating Commission or Concealment Of...

- 121 ALR, Fed. 525, Validity, Construction, and Application of 18 U.S.C.A. § 1956, Which Criminalizes Money Laundering.
- 136 ALR, Fed. 457, What Constitutes "Willfulness" for Purposes of Criminal Provisions of Federal Securities Laws.
- 100 ALR, Fed. 667, Liability, Under Racketeer Influenced and Corrupt Organizations Act (RICO) (18 U.S.C.A. §§ 1961-1968) for Retaliation Against Employee for Disclosing or Refusing to Commit Wrongful Act.
- 43 ALR 6th 1, Circumstances Excusing Demand Upon Board of Directors that is Otherwise Prerequisite to Bringing of Stockholder's Derivative Suit on Behalf of Corporation.
- 18 ALR 5th 1, Actions by State Official Involving Defendant as Constituting "Outrageous" Conduct Violating Due Process Guaranties.
- 23 ALR 5th 241, Excessiveness or Inadequacy of Attorney's Fees in Matters Involving Commercial and General Business Activities.
- 173 ALR 576, Comment Note.--What Constitutes Concealment Which Will Prevent Running of Statute of Limitations.

Encyclopedias

- 32 Am. Jur. Proof of Facts 3d 129, Proving Fraudulent Concealment to Toll Statutory Limitations Periods.
- 4 Am. Jur. Trials 441, Solving Statutes of Limitation Problems.
- Am. Jur. 2d Corporations § 1962, Timing of Demand and Filing of Action.
- Am. Jur. 2d Monopolies, Restraints of Trade, etc. § 497, Accrual of Cause of Action.
- Am. Jur. 2d Securities Regulation-Federal § 271, Prohibitions.
- Am. Jur. 2d Securities Regulation-Federal § 1391, Exchange Act Provisions; Section 10(B) and Sec Rules Thereunder--Foreign Corrupt Practices Act.
- Am. Jur. 2d Securities Regulation-Federal § 1635, Securities Exchange Act Provisions.
- Am. Jur. 2d Securities Regulation-Federal § 1657, Securities Exchange Act.

Treatises and Practice Aids

- Callmann on Unfair Compet., TMs, & Monopolies § 12:1, Introduction.
- Callmann on Unfair Compet., TMs, & Monopolies § 9:27, Competitive Relationships--The Privilege to Compete.
- Callmann on Unfair Compet., TMs, & Monopolies § 27:29, Extraterritorial Application of United States Laws--Lex Loci Delicti (And the Most Significant Relationship).
- Due Diligence in Securities Transactions § 6:26, Standard for Auditing Internal Control Over Financial Reporting--Sec Guidance.
- Eckstrom's Licensing Foreign & Domestic Ops Jt Vent § 6:1, The Current Enforcement Climate.
- Eckstrom's Licensing Foreign & Domestic Ops Jt Vent § 1:39, The Foreign Corrupt Practices Act.
- Eckstrom's Licensing Foreign & Domestic Ops Jt Vent § 6:15, The Foreign Corrupt Practices Act.
- Federal Procedure, Lawyers Edition § 36:555, Action for Injunction by Attorney General.
- Federal Procedure, Lawyers Edition § 36:562, Issuance of Advisory Opinion.
- Restatement (Third) of Foreign Relations § 414, Jurisdiction With Respect to Activities of Foreign Branches and Subsidiaries.
- Sarbanes-Oxley Act in Perspective § 3:14, Commission Implements Section 404 and the Assessment of Internal Control Over Financial Reporting.
- Sarbanes-Oxley Act in Perspective § 8:18, Rule 13b2-2(B)--Improper Influence on Conduct of Audits.
- Securities and Federal Corporate Law § 22:52, Improper and Corrupt Corporate Payments--Corrupt Payments.
- Securities and Federal Corporate Law § 30:42, Rule 13b2-2(B)--Improper Influence on Conduct of Audits.
- Securities and Federal Corporate Law § 7:35.55, Section 404 Assessment of Internal Control Over Financial Reporting.
- 25 Securities and Federal Corporate Law Report 1, Commission in Final Stages of Implementing Sarbanes-Oxley - Part II.

- 25 Securities and Federal Corporate Law Report 1, Commission Determines PCAOB Organized and Operational, Recognizes Fasb as the Standard Setting Board in Final Stages of Implementing Sarbanes-Oxley - Part I.
- Securities Crimes § 6:36, Anti-Bribery Provisions.
- Securities Crimes § 6:37, Anti-Bribery Provisions--Facilitating Payments.
- Securities Crimes § 6:38, Anti-Bribery Provisions--Affirmative Defenses.
- Securities Prac.: Fed. & State Enforcement, 2nd Ed § 4:1, Introduction.
- US Sec. L. Int'L Fin. Trans. & Cap. Markets 2d Ed § 1:4, Statutes--Securities Exchange Act of 1934 (Exchange Act).
- US Sec. L. Int'L Fin. Trans. & Cap. Markets 2d Ed § 6:186, Foreign Corrupt Practices Act.

NOTES OF DECISIONS

- Aiding and abetting 15
- Collateral estoppel 11
- Compromise or settlement 9
- Constitutionality 1/4
- Construction with other laws 1/2
- Corrupt actions 14
- Customs duties and taxes 3
- Discretionary acts, facilitating payments exception 13
- Facilitating payments exception 12, 13

  o Facilitating payments exception - Generally 12
  o Facilitating payments exception - Discretionary acts 13

- Foreign officials 2
- Indictment 5
- Issue preclusion 11
- Jurisdiction 10
- Limitations 6
- Pleadings 8

- Purpose 1
- Scienter 4
- Settlement 9
- Weight and sufficiency of evidence 7

1/4. Constitutionality

Foreign Corrupt Practices Act (FCPA) provision which prohibited bribery of foreign officials was not unconstitutionally vague as applied to officer of offshore drilling company who allegedly provided bribe to Nigerian government official to obtain temporary import permits (TIPs) based on fraudulent documents, since a person of common intelligence would have no difficulty understanding that routine government actions did not include the granting of TIP permits based on false documents. S.E.C. v. Jackson, S.D.Tex.2012, 908 F.Supp.2d 834. Constitutional Law 4509(21); Securities Regulation 2.10

1/2. Construction with other laws

Executives of Hungarian telecommunication company accused of using Greek intermediary to bribe Macedonian government officials had, under Exchange Act, sufficient minimum contacts with the United States to establish prima facie case of personal jurisdiction over them in Securities and Exchange Commission's (SEC) suit alleging violation of Foreign Corrupt Practices Act (FCPA), even though their actions had not been principally directed toward the United States; company's securities were registered with the SEC and publicly traded on the New York Stock Exchange (NYSE), so executives knew, or should have known, that false or misleading financial reports concealing bribes given to foreign officials would influence purchases by prospective American investors. S.E.C. v. Straub, S.D.N.Y.2013, 921 F.Supp.2d 244, motion to certify appeal denied 2013 WL 4399042. Securities Regulation 133

Because employer and other defendants were not issuers, only the Department of Justice (DOJ), and not the Securities and Exchange

Commission (SEC) had jurisdiction over them with respect to Foreign Corrupt Practices Act (FCPA) violations, and consequently, anti-retaliation provision of Dodd-Frank Wall Street Reform and Consumer Protection Act (DFA) did not extend to employee who reported defendants' potential FCPA violations; employee was not a "whistleblower" under the DFA, and the violations reported by employee did not "relate to violations of the securities laws" within meaning of DFA. Nollner v. Southern Baptist Convention, Inc., M.D.Tenn.2012, 2012 WL 1108923. Labor and Employment 819; Securities Regulation 35.14

1. Purpose

Foreign Corrupt Practices Act was primarily designed to protect integrity of American foreign policy and domestic markets, rather than to prevent use of foreign resources to reduce production costs. Lamb v. Phillip Morris, Inc., C.A.6 (Ky.) 1990, 915 F.2d 1024, certiorari denied 111 S.Ct. 961, 498 U.S. 1086, 112 L.Ed.2d 1048. Securities Regulation 67.10

2. Foreign officials

Foreign officials may not be prosecuted under the general conspiracy statute for conspiring to violate the Foreign Corrupt Practices Act (FCPA). U.S. v. Castle, C.A.5 (Tex.) 1991, 925 F.2d 831. International Law 10.25

Securities and Exchange Commission's (SEC) complaint sufficiently alleged bribe of "foreign official," as required to state claim against executives of publicly traded Hungarian telecommunications company for violation of Foreign Corrupt Practices Act (FCPA) based on bribery of Macedonian public officers and resulting false statements in securities filings; allegations included that defendants had used a Greek intermediary to negotiate and further bribery scheme in Macedonia, and since FCPA did not require that identity of foreign officials be pled with specificity, it was not necessary for SEC to provide the names of Macedonian officials who had been bribed, in order to state a claim. S.E.C. v. Straub, S.D.N.Y.2013, 921 F.Supp.2d 244, motion to certify appeal denied 2013 WL 4399042. Securities Regulation 67.13

3.  Customs duties and taxes

    Payments made by the defendants to foreign government officials for purpose of reducing customs duties and taxes did not fall under the scope of provision of the Foreign Corrupt Practices Act (FCPA), prohibiting payments to foreign officials to obtain or retain business; although the plain language of the statute was ambiguous, legislative history showed that the Congress specifically rejected proposed language to broaden the "obtain or retain business" clause that would have covered the defendants' conduct. U.S. v. Kay, S.D.Tex.2002, 200 F.Supp.2d 681, reversed and remanded 359 F.3d 738.

4.  Scienter

    Securities and Exchange Commission's (SEC) complaint sufficiently alleged "use of an instrumentality of interstate commerce," as required to state claim against executives of publicly traded Hungarian telecommunications company for violation of Foreign Corrupt Practices Act (FCPA) based on bribery of Macedonian public officials and resulting false statements in securities filings; allegations included that defendants had used e-mails in furtherance of their bribery scheme by attaching to them protocols and letters of intent related to the scheme, and that such e-mails had been routed through and stored on network servers located within the United States, and since mens rea requirement of statute applied only to the making of bribes, not the use of interstate commerce, SEC was not required to allege defendants' intent to use interstate commerce in order to state claim. S.E.C. v. Straub, S.D.N.Y.2013, 921 F.Supp.2d 244, motion to certify appeal denied 2013 WL 4399042. Securities Regulation 67.13

    Securities and Exchange Commission's (SEC) complaint against officer and internal auditor of offshore drilling company for violations of Foreign Corrupt Practices Act (FCPA) sufficiently alleged defendants' knowledge that charges they authorized the company to pay to customs agent were to be used for bribes to Nigerian officials, as required to state claim for unlawful bribery under FCPA; allegations included that under officer's direction, the company had been sanctioned by the Nigerian government for using false paperwork to obtain temporary import permits (TIPs), that payments to agent for TIPs were cryptically titled as "special handling" or "procurement" charges in company's books and given blanket approval, and that both officer and auditor believed that customs agent was not operating "above the table" and that agent had charged fees in excess of actual cost of TIPs. S.E.C. v. Jackson, S.D.Tex.2012, 908 F.Supp.2d 834. Securities Regulation 67.13

Shareholders' class action securities fraud complaint sufficiently alleged that issuer's officers either knew or were severely reckless in not knowing of overstated sales revenue by inclusion of sales from illegal activities in Asia that violated Foreign Corrupt Practices Act (FCPA), as necessary for issuer's scienter under PSLRA requirements, based on high-level employees making false statements to market as issuer's ongoing method of doing business; complaint alleged that vice president was terminated for his direct involvement in and knowledge of illegal conduct in Asia, that senior manager had knowledge of use of bribes to generate sales in Asia, that ex-company manager for South Korea had additional information about illegal conduct, and that annual report acknowledged improper payments and personnel terminations due to internal investigation of misconduct in Asia. In re Faro Technologies Securities Litigation, M.D.Fla.2007, 534 F.Supp.2d 1248. Securities Regulation 60.51(2)

5. Indictment

Allegations that defendants agreed to violate the Foreign Corrupt Practices Act (FCPA), and that defendant joined the conspiracy with knowledge that bribes had been paid and would continue to be paid to Azeri officials in exchange for ensuring defendants' participation in the privatization of an oil company, were sufficient to support indictment for conspiring to bribe government officials in the Republic of Azerbaijan. U.S. v. Kozeny, S.D.N.Y.2007, 493 F.Supp.2d 693, affirmed 541 F.3d 166. Indictment And Information 10.2(10)

6. Limitations

Where purpose or intent of transporting funds was to violate Foreign Corrupt Practices Act (FCPA), money laundering conspiracy had not terminated for limitations purposes when last transfer of funds occurred since conspirators, who bribed Azeri officials in order to encourage the privatization of Republic of Azerbaijan-owned oil company and reap substantial returns on their voucher investments, had not received any returns on their investments because the privatization had not occurred at that time; rather, conspiracy ended when co-conspirators abandoned their attempts at encouraging the privatization of oil company or when they ceased paying bribes to Azeri officials. U.S. v. Kozeny, S.D.N.Y.2009, 638 F.Supp.2d 348. Criminal Law 150

7. Weight and sufficiency of evidence

Evidence was sufficient to present jury question on defendant's guilt on charge of conspiring to violate the Foreign Corrupt Practices Act (FCPA); evidence showed that defendant's bribes to Azeri officials was to encourage the privatization of Republic of Azerbaijan-owned oil company. U.S. v. Kozeny, S.D.N.Y.2009, 638 F.Supp.2d 348. Bribery 13

8. Pleadings

Securities and Exchange Commission's (SEC) complaint against executives of publicly traded Hungarian telecommunication company for bribery of Macedonian public officials in violation of Foreign Corrupt Practices Act (FCPA) sufficiently linked the fraudulent statements made to the individual defendants accused, rather than utilizing group pleading doctrine, as required to satisfy federal rule for pleading fraud; complaint identified specific statements that were misleading, why they were misleading, which defendant said them, and the SEC filings or audits for which they were made. S.E.C. v. Straub, S.D.N.Y.2013, 921 F.Supp.2d 244, motion to certify appeal denied 2013 WL 4399042. Securities Regulation 67.13

Securities and Exchange Commission's (SEC) complaint against officers of offshore drilling company for violations of Foreign Corrupt Practices Act

(FCPA) sufficiently identified foreign officials, as required to state claim for unlawful bribery under FCPA, even though complaint did not plead with specificity the names or positions of Nigerian officials whom the company had allegedly bribed; complaint alleged that defendants had made payments to "Nigerian government officials" to process eleven illegitimate temporary import permits (TIPs) for offshore drilling based on false paperwork, had obtained discretionary or unlawful extensions of these TIPs, and that such payments had been made to both the Nigerian Port Authority (NPA) and the National Maritime Authority (NMA). S.E.C. v. Jackson, S.D.Tex.2012, 908 F.Supp.2d 834. Securities Regulation 67.13

Shareholders' allegations that corporation enjoyed an increase in international sales and then had an employee indicted for violating the Foreign Corrupt Practices Act (FCPA) were inadequate to justify shareholders' failure to make demand on the corporation's board, as required by Nevada law, prior to filing derivative suit alleging the corporation's board and officers breached their duty of care by failing to prevent FCPA violations; there was no allegation that the board was aware of a long history of criminal activity and failed to act. Holt v. Golden, D.Mass.2012, 880 F.Supp.2d 199. Corporations and Business Organizations 2101

Under Delaware law, shareholder failed to satisfy particularity requirement in pleading that demand was excused in his derivative action against corporation's officers and directors alleging that they failed to adequately oversee compliance and reporting activities that were in violation of Foreign Corrupt Practices Act (FCPA) and Securities Exchange Act; shareholder failed to identify how each officer and director knew that corporation was violating internal controls it had in place for compliance with FCPA and Securities Exchange Act, and he failed to identify when and from whom each officer and director gained such knowledge. Freuler v. Parker, S.D.Tex.2011, 803 F.Supp.2d 630, affirmed 517 Fed.Appx. 227, 2013 WL 1153058. Corporations and Business Organizations 2101

9. Compromise or settlement

Approval of proposed settlement agreement was warranted in Securities and Exchange Commission's (SEC) civil enforcement action alleging violations of anti-bribery and internal controls provisions of Foreign Corrupt Practices Act and of aiding and abetting violations of Investment Advisers Act, even though SEC's proposed settlement apparently did not reflect any restitution that might be owed to victims of defendant's criminal conduct, where defendant had entered guilty plea in parallel criminal prosecution, defendant had limited assets, and defendant's former employer stipulated that it would not seek restitution in criminal case, but reserved right to pursue civil relief in separate proceeding at later date. U.S. v. Peterson, E.D.N.Y.2012, 859 F.Supp.2d 477. Securities Regulation 156

## 10. Jurisdiction

Court's exercise of personal jurisdiction, pursuant to Exchange Act, over executives of Hungarian telecommunications company accused in Securities and Exchange Commission (SEC) suit of using Greek intermediary to bribe Macedonian government officials, in violation of Foreign Corrupt Practices Act (FCPA), would comport with fair play and substantial justice as required to establish prima facie case of personal jurisdiction over them; although it might not have been convenient for defendants to defend action in the United States, there was no alternative forum available for SEC suit, and United States had a strong federal interest in enforcing its securities laws. S.E.C. v. Straub, S.D.N.Y.2013, 921 F.Supp.2d 244, motion to certify appeal denied 2013 WL 4399042. Securities Regulation 133

Even if employer and other defendants violated Foreign Corrupt Practices Act (FCPA) and employee was protected by Tennessee law against retaliation for disclosing those violations, employee's Tennessee retaliatory discharge claim would not involve a federal question over which court could exercise "arising under" jurisdiction. Nollner v. Southern Baptist Convention, Inc., M.D.Tenn.2012, 852 F.Supp.2d 986. Labor and Employment 852

## 11. Issue preclusion

Prior Massachusetts state court decision dismissing derivative suit against corporation based on shareholder's failure to make a pre-suit demand involved identical issue with current derivative suit against corporation brought by different shareholders, which alleged corporation's board and officers breached their duty of care by failing to prevent violations of the Foreign Corrupt Practices Act (FCPA), as required by Massachusetts law to preclude shareholders in current suit from litigating issue of whether it would have been futile for them to make a pre-suit demand on the board, as they were required to do under Nevada law; although the misconduct alleged in the two cases was different, the material issue of the disinterestedness of the board was precisely identical in both cases, and at least four of the seven directors that the state court found were disinterested were still on the board at the time current lawsuit was filed. Holt v. Golden, D.Mass.2012, 880 F.Supp.2d 199. Judgment 828.14(3); Judgment 828.16(1)

12. Facilitating payments exception--Generally

Securities and Exchange Commission's (SEC) complaint against officers of offshore drilling company for unlawful bribery of foreign officials sufficiently alleged that payments company made to Nigerian customs officials for initial temporary import permits (TIPs) based on false paperwork did not fall under facilitating payments exception to Foreign Corrupt Practices Act (FCPA); complaint alleged that company knew payments would be going to Nigerian government officials to obtain TIPs in a manner that violated Nigerian law, and that as such, payments were not merely expediting foreign government's "ministerial" actions. S.E.C. v. Jackson, S.D.Tex.2012, 908 F.Supp.2d 834. Securities Regulation 67.13

13. Discretionary acts, facilitating payments exception

Securities and Exchange Commission's (SEC) complaint against officers of offshore drilling company for unlawful bribery of foreign officials, in violation of Foreign Corrupt Practices Act (FCPA), based on payments company made to Nigerian customs officials for extensions to temporary import permits (TIPs), contained no allegation that a government official's granting of such an extension was discretionary under Nigerian law, as required to show that payment did not fall within facilitating payments exception to FCPA. S.E.C. v. Jackson, S.D.Tex.2012, 908 F.Supp.2d 834. Securities Regulation 67.13

14. Corrupt actions

Securities and Exchange Commission's (SEC) complaint against officers of offshore drilling company for unlawful bribery of foreign officials, based on payments company allegedly made to Nigerian customs officials for initial temporary import permits (TIPs), sufficiently alleged that the officers acted corruptly, as required to state claim under Foreign Corrupt Practices Act (FCPA), by asserting that officers acted with the wrongful purposes of influencing the foreign officials to misuse their positions by submitting bribes along with false paperwork, in contravention of what they knew to be the proper protocol. S.E.C. v. Jackson, S.D.Tex.2012, 908 F.Supp.2d 834. Securities Regulation 67.13

15. Aiding and abetting

Securities and Exchange Commission's (SEC) complaint against officers of offshore drilling company stated claim for aiding and abetting company's bribery of foreign government officials, in violation of Foreign Corrupt Practices Act (FCPA); complaint alleged a primary violation on the basis of payments the company made to obtain temporary import permits (TIPs) from Nigerian officials using fraudulent documents, and sufficiently alleged officers' degree of knowledge of the primary violation based on an agreement to label bribes as "special handling fees" and approve the fees despite knowing they were associated with false paperwork. S.E.C. v. Jackson, S.D.Tex.2012, 908 F.Supp.2d 834. Securities Regulation 67.13

15 U.S.C.A. § 78dd-1, 15 USCA § 78dd-1

Current through P.L. 113-92 (excluding P.L. 113-79 and 113-89) approved 3-25-14

END OF DOCUMENT

ASPATORE